D1487139

LOVE

— & —

SEX

TESTS

LOVE

—&—

SEX

TESTS

**24 REVEALING LOVE, SEX,
AND RELATIONSHIP TESTS
DEVELOPED BY PSYCHOLOGISTS**

LOUIS JANDA, PH.D.

Adams Media Corporation
HOLBROOK, MASSACHUSETTS

Published by
Adams Media Corporation
260 Center Street, Holbrook, MA 02343

ISBN: 1-58062-002-7

Printed in the United States of America.

J I H G F E D C B A

Library of Congress Cataloging-in-Publication Data

Janda, Louis H.
    Love & sex tests : twenty-four psychological tests to help you evaluate
your readiness for relationships, love, and sex / Louis H. Janda.
    p.   cm.
    ISBN 1-58062-002-7
    1. Love—Testing—Handbooks, manuals, etc. 2. Sex (Psychology)—
Testing—Handbooks, manuals, etc. I. Title.
BF575.L8J35   1998
306.7'076—dc21   98-20209
                                                                      CIP

This publication is designed to provide accurate and authoritative information with regard to the subject matter covered. It is sold with the understanding that the publisher is not engaged in rendering legal, accounting, or
other professional advice. If legal advice or other expert assistance is
required, the services of a competent professional person should be sought.
    —From a *Declaration of Principles* jointly adopted by a Committee of the
American Bar Association and a Committee of Publishers and Associations

Cover photo ©TSM/Norbert Schäfer, 1996.

*This book is available at quantity discounts for bulk purchases.
For information, call 1-800-872-5627 (in Massachusetts, 781-767-8100).*

Visit our home page at http://www.adamsmedia.com

To the most important person in my life,
Meredith

Contents

Part III: Making Love 115

Part IV: Making Love Last 175

Prologue

THE ART AND SCIENCE OF RELATIONSHIPS

A few years ago, my neighbors' daughter became engaged to be married. Susan, then in her early thirties, was deliriously happy about her prospective marriage. She had had a number of serious relationships, but none had worked out. She desperately wanted children and was becoming frightened that time would pass her by. Susan was anxious to start her new life and her new family.

Her parents, on the other hand, were less than enthusiastic about their daughter's engagement. While they wanted Susan to have her own family, they had serious reservations about her fiancé, Michael. Michael and Susan met shortly after Michael separated from his first wife. After seeing each other every day for two weeks, Michael declared his undying love for Susan and announced his desire to marry her as soon as his divorce became final. Michael was a well-educated man who seemed to be on his way up in a large corporation, but he and his first wife had lived well beyond their means. The separation left Michael saddled with debt, and Susan had to pay for most of their evenings out.

Michael had two young children, and he took his responsibility to them very seriously. Unfortunately for Susan, the children resented her; they believed she was responsible for their parents' divorce, and they were not shy about letting her know how they felt. His children's complaints filled Michael with guilt, so when the four of them were together, he was determined to prove to his children that they were more important to him than Susan was. It particularly galled Susan (to say nothing of her parents) that when in the car, the children sat in the front seat with Michael while Susan sat alone in the back seat.

Michael talked often about his need to unwind from the tension of his job and divorce proceedings, and his favorite way to do so was to have, in his words, a few drinks. More often than not, a few drinks turned into most of a bottle of scotch. Susan had become proficient at undressing her half-conscious fiancé and putting him to bed. On two occasions, while "unwinding" at parties, Michael was seen kissing other women in more than just a friendly way. Susan was both hurt and embarrassed by his behavior but excused it as a symptom of the stress he was experiencing. She was convinced that once they were married, he would no longer feel a need to engage in such unacceptable conduct.

Susan's parents were plenty worried by what they saw in Michael, but their fears were compounded by their concern with Susan's level of maturity. Susan was a talented artist, and her parents were more than happy to have her move back home after she finished college so that she could devote herself to her work without having to worry about paying bills. But "a year or two" turned into a decade, and Susan had shown no signs of wanting to go out on her own. She was very comfortable in the loft her parents had built for her, and while she sold enough of her work to make the payments on her BMW, she couldn't begin to support herself in the style to which she felt entitled. Her parents saw no alternative other than for Susan to find a regular job to help Michael recover from the financial devastation of his divorce, but Susan talked about spending her days preparing gourmet meals for her new husband and decorating their apartment. Susan also refused to talk about her relationship with Michael's children. She dismissed their hostility and cheerily asserted that they would come to love her once they realized she was not going away.

It didn't take a Ph.D. in psychology to realize that Susan and Michael didn't have much of a chance. Her parents had shared their concerns with several people in our neighborhood, and the consensus was that Susan would be back home within a year. As it turned out, she moved back to her parents' house six months after the wedding.

Why was Susan so oblivious to what was painfully obvious to everyone else? Clearly, she is not alone. Most of us have had the experience of viewing a romantic partner through rose-colored glasses. Susan's glasses simply had a darker tint than most.

The problem most of us have is that emotion plays a substantial role in our choice of a romantic partner— sometimes to the point where it impairs our ability to be rational. This certainly happened to Susan. Six months after she left Michael, she wondered how she ever could have believed their marriage would possibly work. But at the time, her emotions were so intense that she simply could not process information that suggested anything negative about their relationship. She was deeply in love with him. She had an intense longing for children of her own. She was consumed with visions of being the perfect wife and stepmother while achieving the success as an artist that she ardently craved. She wanted it all, and her new husband would help her to get it. It was almost as if Michael was a drug and she was addicted to the high. Indeed, some researchers have implicated phenylethylamine, an amphetamine-like, natural brain chemical often referred to as PEA, as producing the high that we call love. And those addicted to this chemically induced high find it difficult to act rationally and logically.

Even when our PEA levels are running wild, most of us retain enough of our objectivity so that, unlike Susan, we can avoid egregious mistakes. I have known people who canceled their weddings when they learned that their partners were sexually involved with someone else. And I've known a number of people who ended their relationships when their partners showed the slightest signs of physical violence or substance abuse.

But most of us have our blind spots. I know that my PEA level made it impossible for me to be completely rational about marrying Meredith, my wife. We had different views about religion and different visions of our future. Luckily, we were able to work out these differences, and we are well into our third decade of marriage. But had either of us been less flexible, any one of these differences (and probably a dozen more that I cannot remember) could have meant the end of our marriage.

So what are you to do if your blind spots make it difficult for you to find the right person? And what about those times when you believe you've found someone with whom you can have a future, but it becomes nearly impossible to make the relationship work? That is where this book comes in. Within these pages, you will find twenty-four psychological tests that are relevant to having satisfying and lasting relationships. By completing these tests and analyzing the results, it is hoped that you will be able to identify a few of the blind spots that keep you from finding the right person and, once you do find Mr. or Ms. Right, make the relationship work.

The book is divided into four parts, each of which includes six psychological tests. Part I, Being Prepared for Love, is comprised of tests that measure qualities that are relevant to the ability to form relationships and make them work. When we think of finding that perfect love, most of us think about meeting the right person. And when a relationship goes badly, we talk to our friends endlessly about our lovers' flaws. But the reality is that we must be socially competent if we are to have any chance of meeting the person right for us, and we must be relatively well adjusted if we are to have any chance of making the relationship work. The six tests in Part I will provide you with a sense of whether you are prepared for the time when you do meet Mr. or Ms. Right.

Part II, Falling in Love, is comprised of six tests that reflect a variety of aspects of romantic love. These tests will provide you with insight as to how you experience romantic love and how your feelings of love may influence your perceptions and your behavior. After you complete these six tests, you will have learned something about the tint in your rose-colored glasses.

The six tests in Part III, Making Love, will allow you to thoroughly understand your sexuality. Sex is a curious phenomenon. Early in a relationship, it usually seems to be the easiest thing in the world for two people to enjoy sharing. But for many couples, it is difficult to sustain that early excitement over the course of a long-term relationship. These tests will provide you with information about your sexuality that you might benefit by exploring. Also, they will provide ideas as to how you could communicate with your partner more effectively about your sexual relationship.

Part IV, Making Love Last, is comprised of six tests for people who have found Mr. or Ms. Right and want to ensure that this relationship can withstand the test of time. Relationships are always a work in progress. Because both our interests and our situations change, there are continual new challenges that must be met. The tests in this section may help you deal more effectively with problems that have undermined all too many relationships.

An ideal strategy for using this book is for both you and your partner to take the tests and to compare your scores. Should your partner decline (or if you are not far enough along in your relationship to ask), take the test for your partner, and respond to the items as you believe he or she would. This will make it possible for you to learn about potential trouble spots in your relationship. You should keep in mind, however, that often we do not view ourselves in the same ways in which we are viewed by others. Your partner might respond to the tests very differently than you believe he or she would.

Psychologists have learned a great deal about love, sex, and marriage over the past several decades; enough so that it is legitimate to use the phrase *the science of romantic relationships*. We can identify a number of human characteristics that are related to people getting together in the first place and a number of additional personal qualities that are related to relationship satisfaction. We can predict at a better than chance level which relationships are likely to stand the test of time and which will not. This book is intended to help you utilize this science so that you can have a relationship that is happier, more satisfying, and enduring.

Keep in mind, though, that the science of relationships is far from exact. It is impossible to put a number on the precision with which relationship satisfaction can be predicted. But if I had to guess, I would say that couples who went for a thorough psychological evaluation prior to making a commitment and followed their psychologist's advice could improve their odds of staying together from fifty-fifty to two-in-three, possibly three-in-four. While this would result in a substantial reduction in the divorce rate, it still leaves plenty of room for error. Despite using the best information our science of romantic relationships has to offer, our predictions would still mean that from one fourth to one third of all couples who appeared to be a good match would nonetheless eventually part ways. Our science of romantic relationships would also lead us to advise many other couples, who could have had a good relationship had they tried, to find more suitable partners. To borrow from medical terminology, predictions based on the science of romantic relationships would have substantial numbers of both false positives and false negatives.

The important point to keep in mind is that these tests should be used as a vehicle for discussion, as a guide for exploring various issues. They should not, under any circumstances, be used as the sole basis for making a decision about the viability of a relationship. No psychological test, regardless of how strong its scientific basis may be, is precise enough to allow for such certainty.

Had Meredith, my wife, relied solely on these tests to decide whether I would make a suitable husband, we might not know each other today. While the tests would have pointed to many things we had going for us, they also would have revealed some serious differences and more than a few of my flaws. I'm not sure how rational and objective either of us were in evaluating our differences, but somehow we were able to work them out.

The critical point to keep in mind is that the information gained from the results of these tests is just one source of information you have about yourself and your partner. Think about your feelings and what you want from a relationship. Pay attention to your partner's reaction when a test reveals a potentially troublesome area. And most of all, be honest with yourself and your partner when you discuss these issues. There is no magical tool that can guarantee that you will find the right person and make your relationship last, but these tests can help to lighten the tint on your rose-colored glasses.

Good luck, and have fun.

A FEW WORDS ABOUT THE TESTS

All of the tests in this book are true psychological tests. This means that they were developed by behavioral scientists familiar with scientific principles of test construction and that the authors of the tests collected data to ensure that their instruments were reliable and valid.

While all of the tests in this book have clear practical applications, most of them were developed to be used in behavioral research rather than as clinical tools. This means that while test scores can distinguish between groups of people, they were not intended to be used to make absolute judgments about people. So, while a test may be useful in predicting, say, which individuals are likely to have a lasting relationship, none of the tests here were meant to be used to arrive at conclusions like "this person is poor marriage material." The tests reveal individual differences among people, but they were not developed to place people in categories, nor should they be used in that way.

For each test, I will provide you with five reference points that can be used to provide a sense of how you compare with others. These reference points, or norms as they are called by psychologists, are the percentile scores of 15, 30, 50, 70, and 85. A percentile score is simply the percentage of people who can be expected to receive lower scores on the test. So, a percentile score of 15 means that 15 percent of people can be expected to receive lower scores, and a percentile score of 70 means that 70 percent of people can be expected to receive lower scores on the test.

The norms provided with each test should only be thought of as a rough guideline as to how you compare with others. In most cases, the men and women upon whose responses the norms are based were students at the university with which the test's author was affiliated. If you are older than the typical college student, for example, your greater experience may influence your responses. The norms will provide you with a good sense of how you compare with others, but keep in mind that your percentile scores might have been somewhat different had the normative group consisted of people similar to yourself.

Okay. You're ready to get started. Keep an open mind, be honest, and most of all, remember that these tests are to be used as a tool for you to learn more about yourself and your partner. I hope you enjoy the process, and I hope this book will help you find a fulfilling and lasting relationship.

Being Prepared for Love

After taking the tests in Part I, you will know whether you have any personal qualities that are standing in the way of meeting potential partners and forming relationships with them. The following tests are included in Part I:

CHAPTER ONE

The UCLA Loneliness Scale— Version 3

The following statements describe how people sometimes feel. For each statement, please indicate how often you feel the way described by writing a number in the space provided. For example, consider this question: How often do you feel happy? If you never felt happy, you would respond with a 1, indicating "never"; if you always feel happy, you would respond with a 4, indicating "always."

1 = Never
2 = Rarely
3 = Sometimes
4 = Always

---

* Reprinted with permission of Dr. Daniel W. Russell, Center for Family Research in Rural Mental Heath, Iowa State University, Ames, Iowa.

___ 1. How often do you feel that you are "in tune" with the people around you?

___ 2. How often do you feel that you lack companionship?

___ 3. How often do you feel that there is no one you can turn to?

___ 4. How often do you feel alone?

___ 5. How often do you feel part of a group of friends?

___ 6. How often do you feel that you have a lot in common with the people around you?

___ 7. How often do you feel that you are no longer close to anyone?

___ 8. How often do you feel that your interests and ideas are not shared by those around you?

___ 9. How often do you feel outgoing and friendly?

___ 10. How often do you feel close to people?

___ 11. How often do you feel left out?

___ 12. How often do you feel that your relationships with others are not meaningful?

___ 13. How often do you feel that no one really knows you well?

___ 14. How often do you feel isolated from others?

___ 15. How often do you feel you can find companionship when you want it?

___ 16. How often do you feel that there are people who really understand you?

___ 17. How often do you feel shy?

___ 18. How often do you feel that people are around you but not with you?

1 = Never; 2 = Rarely; 3 = Sometimes; 4 = Always

___ 19. How often do you feel that there are people you can talk to?

___ 20. How often do you feel that there are people you can turn to?

SCORING

Before you add your total score, you must reverse the scores on the following items: 1, 5, 6, 9, 10, 15, 16, 19, and 20. The guidelines for doing this are 1 = 4, 2 = 3, 3 = 2, and 4 = 1.

HOW DO YOU COMPARE?

SCORE	PERCENTILE
49	85
44	70
40	50
36	30
31	15

High scores indicate greater loneliness. If you received a score of 70, for instance, it means that 70 percent of people scored lower than you did in level of loneliness.

For more information about the UCLA Loneliness Scale (Version 3), see Daniel W. Russell, "UCLA Loneliness Scale (Version 3): Reliability, Validity, and Factor Structure," *Journal of Personality Assessment* 66 (1996): 20–40.

ABOUT THE UCLA LONELINESS SCALE

Since social relationships are at the core of human life, it is surprising that until recently, research psychologists have paid little attention to the problem of loneliness. Clinicians have known for some time that loneliness is common and that often it is at the core of a number of other problems. Surveys have found that as many as one fourth of people report feeling very lonely at any point in time, and mental health professionals have observed that loneliness is often linked with problems such as alcoholism, suicide, and even physical illnesses. Despite these observations, it was not until Dan Russell introduced the initial version of the UCLA Loneliness Scale twenty years ago that researchers began to explore exactly what it meant to be lonely. Russell's scale provided scientists with a reliable means of measuring this emotional state. Over the years, Russell has refined his scale and collected extensive data supporting its validity. The most recent version was published in 1996 and is called the UCLA Loneliness Scale—Version 3.

Loneliness has come to be viewed as an emotional state that may reflect several problems and interpersonal deficits. The first and perhaps most obvious of these is depression. While not all lonely people are depressed, there is a strong tendency for the two to go together.

Second is poor self-esteem. Lonely people do not feel good about themselves, in part because they are their own worst critics. One simple experiment required lonely people to spend a few minutes talking to a partner whom they had not met previously. Afterwards, lonely people rated their own interpersonal skills lower than their partners rated them. Lonely people also proved to be a critical lot in that they rated their partner's skills lower than the partners rated themselves. There may be something to the cliché that you have to like yourself before you can like others.

Lonely people also tend to be shy, introverted, nonassertive people. They tend to be more anxious than the average person, and they are especially sensitive to criticism or rejection. Indeed, they may find rejection when it does not even exist. While most of us might be disappointed if we asked a friend to go to a movie and were told no, we would probably accept our friend's plea of "too much work" or "other plans." Lonely people tend to see such explanations as a polite way of saying, "I don't want to spend any time with you."

It is certainly not the case that lonely people have all of these qualities, but the odds are great that they have at least a few. This perspective is so important because we probably have a tendency to blame our loneliness on the situation we find ourselves in. We may say we are lonely because we moved to a new city and cannot meet anyone interesting. Or we may feel lonely because we believe the people we know are not nice enough, or accepting enough, or have some other deficit that makes them unsuitable companions. The reality, as harsh as it may sound, is that the first place to look when we are feeling lonely is toward ourselves.

Felicia suffers from loneliness because of her shyness and sensitivity to rejection. She had a small circle of close friends in high school and was quite happy, but none of these friends accompanied her to the college of her choice. She felt overwhelmed her first week on campus. She was surrounded by strangers, and her anxiety made it impossible to break down the barrier that she felt was keeping her from making new friends. Felicia was taken under the wing of her roommate, who invited her to come along to parties and arranged several blind dates for her. But Felicia inevitably felt worse after these encounters. Her shyness made it difficult for her to talk with her dates, and they, in turn, concluded she was not interested in them. Felicia, believing everyone could see her shyness on her face, concluded her dates did not like her. She found it less painful to spend her evenings alone in her room or at the library.

Ed is a very different type of lonely person. He is moderately extroverted and has no difficulty in talking with people. But Ed, who suspects he is not as smart as other people, compensates by telling anyone and everyone how they could do whatever they are doing better if only they would listen to his ideas. His wife left him after a brief marriage because she could not tolerate his critical nature. Ed does not know a single person he can call to go with him to a ball game or a movie. Though he meets women easily, it is rare that one will go out with him more than once or twice.

Ed and Felicia are very different kinds of people, but they have more in common than their loneliness. They share the belief that they could be happy if only they were in a different situation or if only they could meet the right person. Felicia has applied to transfer to a smaller school with the hope that she will meet friendlier people, and Ed continues to move from apartment complex to apartment complex hoping to meet women who are not so afraid of making a commitment. They both would have more success in overcoming their loneliness if they would take a close look at themselves.

Psychological research that finds that lonely people have qualities that make it difficult for them to connect with others does not mean that they are to be blamed for their loneliness. After all, we all have our blind spots, and few of us are so well adjusted that we know exactly how others perceive us. But if lonely people are to have satisfying relationships, they must be prepared to take a hard look at themselves and be willing to take on the arduous work of changing those qualities that are getting in their way. The odds are that they will not find a solution by changing their situation. Russell found that when lonely people were retested after one year, their scores on his test closely paralleled their scores of a year before.

If you received a score at the 85 percentile or above, the first idea you must accept is that it is not necessary to go through life feeling so isolated and alone. It is possible to do something about your feelings. A good place to begin is by taking the five additional tests in this section. They measure individual characteristics that are pertinent to the ability to form relationships. These tests may provide important clues about what you could change about yourself to make it easier to connect with that someone special. If, after taking these tests, you still do not have a clear idea as to what is getting in your way, ask a close friend—or, better yet, a former romantic partner—to help you out. Sometimes it is easier for others to view us objectively than it is for us to do it ourselves. This may seem like a formidable task, but if you sincerely ask for someone's help, the odds are good that it will be forthcoming.

Finally, here is one last thought about loneliness. I've often heard it said that one should not begin a romantic relationship when one is feeling lonely. While I have never seen any research evidence to support this piece of advice, it does make good sense to me. I believe that a relationship has a much better chance of succeeding if both partners enter into it feeling good about themselves and their lives. Relationships that begin as an attempt to fill some emptiness will almost always come up short. Until one learns to fill the emptiness in himself or herself, it will be extremely difficult for anyone else to.

CHAPTER TWO

The Trust Scale

Read each of the following statements and decide whether it is true of your relationship with your partner. Indicate how strongly you agree or disagree by choosing the appropriate number from the scale and placing it in the space provided in the left-hand margin.

1 = Strongly disagree
2 = Moderately disagree
3 = Mildly disagree
4 = Neutral
5 = Mildly agree
6 = Moderately agree
7 = Strongly agree

* Reprinted by permission of Dr. John Rempel, University of Waterloo, Waterloo, Ontario, Canada.

____ 1. I know how my partner is going to act. My partner can always be counted on to act as I expect.

____ 2. I have found that my partner is a thoroughly dependable person, especially when it comes to things that are important.

____ 3. My partner's behavior tends to be quite variable. I can't always be sure what my partner will surprise me with next.

____ 4. Though times may change and the future is uncertain, I have faith that my partner will always be ready and willing to offer me strength, come what may.

____ 5. Based on past experience, I cannot, with complete confidence, rely on my partner to keep promises made to me.

____ 6. It is sometimes difficult for me to be absolutely certain that my partner will always continue to care for me; the future holds too many uncertainties and too many things can change in our relationship as time goes on.

____ 7. My partner is a very honest person, and even if my partner were to make unbelievable statements, people should feel confident that what they are hearing is the truth.

____ 8. My partner is not very predictable. People can't always be certain how my partner is going to act from one day to another.

____ 9. My partner has proven to be a faithful person. No matter who my partner was married to, she or he would never be unfaithful, even if there were absolutely no chance of being caught.

1 = Strongly disagree; 2 = Moderately disagree; 3 = Mildly disagree;
4 = Neutral; 5 = Mildly agree; 6 = Moderately agree; 7 = Strongly agree

___ 10. I am never concerned that unpredictable conflicts and serious tensions may damage our relationship because I know we can weather any storm.

___ 11. I am very familiar with the patterns of behavior my partner has established, and he or she will behave in certain ways.

___ 12. If I have never faced a particular issue with my partner before, I occasionally worry that he or she won't take my feelings into account.

___ 13. Even in familiar circumstances, I am not totally certain my partner will act the same way twice.

___ 14. I feel completely secure in facing unknown new situations because I know my partner will never let me down.

___ 15. My partner is not necessarily someone others always consider reliable. I can think of some times when my partner could not be counted on.

___ 16. I occasionally find myself feeling uncomfortable with the emotional investment I have made in our relationship because I find it hard to completely set aside my doubts about what lies ahead.

___ 17. My partner has not always proven to be trustworthy in the past, and there are times when I am hesitant to let my partner engage in activities that make me feel vulnerable.

___ 18. My partner behaves in a consistent manner.

1 = Strongly disagree; 2 = Moderately disagree; 3 = Mildly disagree;
4 = Neutral; 5 = Mildly agree; 6 = Moderately agree; 7 = Strongly agree

SCORING

Nine of the items on the Trust Scale are reverse scored. This means that you must convert your response to a new number. The guidelines for doing this are 1 = 7, 2 = 6, 3 = 5, 4 = 4, 5 = 3, 6 = 2, and 7 = 1.

The nine items that are reverse scored are 3, 5, 6, 8, 12, 13, 15, 16, and 17. After reversing your responses to these items, simply add together the numbers you assigned to all items.

HOW DO YOU COMPARE?

TOTAL SCORE	PERCENTILE
110	85
105	70
100	50
95	30
90	15

High scores indicate higher levels of trust. If your percentile score was 30, for example, it means that 30 percent of people scored lower than you did in their level of trust.

For more information, see John K. Rempel and John G. Holmes (1986). "How Do I Trust Thee?" *Psychology Today* (February 1996): 28–34.

ABOUT THE TRUST SCALE

Romantic relationships are a partnership, and like any partnership, the two people involved must trust each other if they are to make it work. Indeed, psychologists have called trust one of the cornerstones of an ideal relationship.

Despite the importance that so many philosophers, as well as clinicians, have attributed to the role of trust in relationships, it has not been until relatively recently that research psychologists became interested in this critical quality. John Rempel and John Holmes were among the first to attempt to quantify trust. Their work resulted in the Trust Scale, designed specifically to measure the level of trust between partners in romantic relationships.

They argued that trust is comprised of three components. First, there is the element of predictability. We can have confidence in a predictable partner because we can anticipate what he or she will do in the future. Although unpredictable partners can make life interesting, they have the unfortunate habit of making life unpleasant. If you cannot count on your partner to pay the electric bill or to meet you at your parents' house for dinner, it would be impossible to share any responsibilities or to make any plans. Predictability as an element of trust, however, is more than consistency. As Rempel and Holmes pointed out, many people have extremely consistent partners and are miserable as a result. The partner who drinks too much and passes out at every party is consistent but is unlikely to inspire trust. Trust develops from the confidence that your partner can be counted on to make positive contributions to the relationship.

Dependability, the confidence that you can rely on your partner when it really counts, is the second element of trust. People who have this type of trust can afford to be vulnerable. They know that when they are feeling hurt or rejected, they can confide in their partner and will receive support in return. A dependable partner can be relied on to keep his or her promises.

Predictability and dependability grow from experience. If you learn over time that you can count on your partner to share the responsibilities of the relationship, if experience tells you your partner is truthful with you and keeps all promises, then you have good reason to believe that he or she will behave similarly in the future. But the reality is that both people and situations change. Many a marriage has been rock solid for years, even decades, and then something happens. One partner may have a midlife crisis or meet someone new, and suddenly this person you have counted on for much of your life is no longer there. The ability to put such uncertainties aside comprises the third element of trust, faith. It allows us to go beyond what our experiences tell us and provides us with the security of knowing we can plan a future together.

Rempel and Holmes described the nature of relationships of couples who varied in their level of trust for each other. The high trust group, reflected in a score at about the 70th percentile and above, believed they were involved in a very successful relationship and that their love for their partners was very strong. They saw each other as accepting, caring, and tolerant, and even when they had conflicts, they had the confidence that their partners would listen to what they had to say and respond in a positive way. Interestingly, even after having serious arguments, they concluded that their partners reacted positively. It seemed that they were almost immune to any negative evidence about their partners. Rempel and Holmes speculated that this was possible because their trust, and especially their faith, kept them from attaching too much significance to any particular negative event. They were always willing to give their partners the benefit of the doubt, and even when the partner reacted badly, it was not taken as evidence that he or she did not care about the relationship.

The low trust group, characterized by scores at the 30th percentile and below, had fragile relationships. They reported many problems, were poorly adjusted, and were dissatisfied with their relationships. In contrast to the high trust group, these people did not see their partners as being unselfish, and in the face of conflicts, they anticipated that their partners would react in a critical, defensive, and angry fashion. These people reported a history of broken promises and emotional disappointments, so they had little basis for believing their relationships would ever be satisfying. They had come to expect the worst from their partners.

The middle group, those with scores between the 30th and 70th percentiles, were the most interesting people, according to Rempel and Holmes. Their relationships could be characterized as generally good but with room for improvement. They believed their partners had positive motives, but when they had disagreements, they, like the low trust group, did not expect their partners to respond in a helpful or positive way. But curiously, even though their partners often responded with defensiveness and anger, these people still hung on to the belief that their partners' underlying motives were positive.

These people were especially diligent in finding clues as to what their partners "really" felt about the relationship. They were especially quick to read meaning into both positive and negative acts. Rempel and

Holmes characterized this group as experiencing hopeful trust. They wanted to see the best in their partners, but somehow they were afraid to believe that they would. It was as if they were saying, "Sure, my partner will always love me . . . I hope."

What happens when trust is lost? According to Rempel and Holmes, trust is extremely difficult to get back once it is lost. Even when a partner who has behaved in untrustworthy ways turns over a new leaf and rededicates himself or herself to the relationship, the partner will be unusually diligent in searching for clues that portend additional disappointments. Even when there is clear evidence that the relationship is improving, this is not likely to be viewed as a sign that the untrustworthy partner's motives have changed. And even the most minor slipups will be viewed as evidence that nothing has really changed. Trust can be regained, but it is likely to be a long, arduous process. The moral is clear: One should not risk destroying a partner's trust in the first place.

Trust is something that generally results from experience, but some people are more inclined to be trusting than are others. Some psychologists have speculated that the ability to trust others has its origins in the first year of life, when we learn whether we can trust our parents to meet our needs. Theoretical considerations aside, people who find it difficult to trust a romantic partner may drive a partner away. The man, for instance, who cannot feel confident about his wife's fidelity is likely to make unfounded accusations every time she arrives home a few minutes late or every time she enjoys a conversation with another man. Needless to say, most people strongly dislike being unjustly

accused of some imagined misbehavior. If they conclude that their partner will never learn to trust them,
they may opt to leave the relationship.

Rempel and Holmes offered a few suggestions for
such people. They should guard against overinterpret-
ing negative behavior. If your partner forgets your
birthday and goes off to spend the day with friends, it
is evidence of inconsiderate behavior, but it is not necessarily evidence of a lack of caring about the relationship. On the other hand, be both sensitive and
appreciative of your partner's positive behavior.
Untrusting people are likely to ignore ten instances of
positive behavior and focus instead on the one instance
of negative behavior. By making an effort to notice
what is good about your partner and expressing your
appreciation, you may come to feel more confident
about the bond that exists between the two of you.

CHAPTER THREE

The Revised Shyness Scale

Please read each of the following items carefully, and decide to what extent each is characteristic of your feelings and behavior. Fill in the blank next to each item by choosing a number from the scale provided.

1 = Very uncharacteristic or untrue, strongly disagree
2 = Uncharacteristic
3 = Neutral
4 = Characteristic
5 = Very characteristic or true, strongly agree

---

* Reprinted with permission of Dr. Jonathan Cheek, Wellesley College, Wellesley, Massachusetts.

____ 1. I feel tense when I'm with people I don't know well.

____ 2. I am socially somewhat awkward.

____ 3. I do not find it difficult to ask other people for information.

____ 4. I am often uncomfortable at parties and other social functions.

____ 5. When in a group of people, I have trouble thinking of the right things to talk about.

____ 6. It does *not* take me long to overcome my shyness in new situations.

____ 7. It is hard for me to act natural when I am meeting with new people.

____ 8. I feel nervous when speaking to someone in authority.

____ 9. I have *no* doubts about my social competence.

____ 10. I have trouble looking someone right in the eye.

____ 11. I feel inhibited in social situations.

____ 12. I do *not* find it hard to talk to strangers.

____ 13. I am more shy with members of the opposite sex.

1 = Strongly disagree; 2 = Uncharacteristic; 3 = Neutral;
4 = Characteristic; 5 = Strongly agree

SCORING

Before summing your answers to calculate your total score, it is first necessary to reverse the scores on a few items. These items are 3, 6, 9, and 12. To reverse your responses on these items, perform the following substitutions: 1 = 5, 2 = 4, 3 = 3, 4 = 2, and 5 = 1.

HOW DO YOU COMPARE?

MALE	FEMALE	PERCENTILE
41	40	85
37	36	70
33	32	50
29	28	30
25	24	15

High scores indicate greater shyness. If, for example, you received a score at the 50th percentile, it means that 50 percent of people scored lower than you did in level of shyness.

For more information, see Jonathan M. Cheek and Arnold H. Buss, "Shyness and Sociability," *Journal of Personality and Social Psychology* 41 (1981): 330–339.

ABOUT THE SHYNESS SCALE

Surveys have found that as many as 40 percent of adults suffer from shyness. The term *suffer* is not chosen lightly—people who identify themselves as shy have little difficulty in listing the problems they experience as a result of their social reticence. Among these are difficulty in meeting new people, feelings of depression, loneliness, and isolation, and an inability to think clearly and communicate effectively when meeting new people. The problems of the shy are often compounded because others are likely to misinterpret their behavior. A shy woman, for instance, may spend her time at a party, sitting alone, clutching her drink, hoping that someone will come up and talk to her. Others at the party may wonder, "What makes her think she's too good for the rest of us?" The shy man may suffer through meetings at work trying to summon the courage to express his ideas, but despite his torment, his colleagues may say to each other, "He hasn't had an idea of his own since he came to work here." Shy people tend to believe that their shyness is obvious to the rest of the world, but often the rest of the world sees them as aloof, unsociable, dull, or conceited.

In the realm of romantic relationships, shyness appears to be much more of a handicap for men than for women. A few years ago, I conducted a large-scale survey of single men and women; they answered more than one hundred questions about their dating, love, and sex experiences. One item simply asked if the respondents considered themselves to be shy. Surprisingly, being shy had no relation to a woman's quality or quantity of romantic experiences. Shy women dated as frequently and with as much variety, had as many sexual partners, and enjoyed being single just as much as their nonshy sisters. Compared with their nonshy brothers, however, shy men were not a happy group. They dated infrequently, they had few sexual experiences, and they were extremely unhappy with their single status. Many of them desperately wanted to be married, but their shyness made it difficult for them to meet women with whom they could explore such a possibility. In an especially poignant letter, one thirty-two-year-old man, who clearly suffered from extreme shyness, said that he often had fantasies of simply finding a woman he could talk with on a regular basis.

Other responses to the survey made it clear why shyness is so much more difficult for men than women. Despite everything we have heard about traditional notions regarding sex roles coming to an end, it still remains the case that men continue to be the ones who have to do the asking. Women, for the most part, continue to wait to be asked. A substantial majority of the women in the survey indicated that they felt it was not appropriate for them to approach a strange man to whom they were attracted at places such as a grocery or bookstore. As long as shy women went to places where there were single men, sooner or later one of these men would approach them. Shy men, on the other hand, could not bring themselves to make that initial contact.

The work of psychologists Jonathan Cheek and Arnold Buss, who constructed the Shyness Scale presented here, is especially interesting because the authors added a new wrinkle to the way shyness is conceptualized. They provided evidence that indicates that shyness and sociability are relatively independent. Sociability refers to a desire to be with other people; shyness involves fear and anxiety about social contacts. Contrary to what psychologists have traditionally believed, some shy people are sociable, and some non-shy people are unsociable. Shy but sociable people have the most difficult time in novel social situations. They want to connect with others and to enjoy relationships, but their fear makes it ever so difficult for them to do so. Interestingly, shy-nonsociable people are no more uncomfortable in novel social situations than are nonshys. Shy-nonsociable people do not dazzle anyone with their interpersonal skills, but their low need for social contacts leaves them unconcerned about their lackluster social performance.

Cheek and Buss speculated as to how one could become a shy but sociable person and came to the conclusion that heredity plays an important role. Both fearfulness and sociability have been shown to have a genetic component. But, according to Cheek and Buss, socialization experiences are also important. So, even if one has the genes that predispose him or her to shyness, it does not mean that such a person must go through life afraid to initiate a romantic relationship. Indeed, shyness is one problem that does respond well to both psychotherapy and self-help programs.

If you received a high score on this scale and you believe that your feelings of shyness are making it difficult to form or to enjoy romantic relationships, it would be worth your while to make a systematic attempt to conquer your feelings of shyness. The basic principle behind any self-help or professional program is to make a series of small changes so that you can become increasingly comfortable in even the most challenging social situations. Here are a few ideas about how you can start.

First, make an attempt to appear more friendly and approachable. Begin by practicing smiling in front of the mirror. Next, simply smile at people—especially those of the other sex—whom you come in contact with. Smile at people while you are waiting for an elevator at work or school, smile at people when you get in line at the checkout counter at the grocery store, and smile at people you cross paths with on the sidewalk. You might be surprised by the reaction you get. I'm willing to bet that within a few days, you will begin to perceive the world as a much friendlier place.

Second, after you feel comfortable with your new, more pleasant persona, say a few words to the people you have been smiling at. A simple, "Good morning. How are you today?" will help you become accustomed to talking to strangers, and it may turn out to be that critical icebreaker. I once had a twenty-year-old client who found his first girlfriend after this simple step. After two consecutive "good mornings" while waiting for an elevator, the girl he spoke to asked him what class he was going to. He was so anxious that he couldn't remember exactly what happened, but before she got off the elevator, they had agreed to meet for coffee after class.

The third step is to practice your "small talk" skills. Many shy people complain that they can't think of anything to say to people they meet for the first time. But the simple truth is that it doesn't much matter what you say. No matter how trite or tired your comment may be, it still serves the purpose of breaking the ice. "Sure is hot today," is not high on the cleverness scale, but it gives the other person the opportunity to respond. Many of these people may offer a simple, "Sure is," and turn away, but as long as you regularly offer others the opportunity to talk to you, you will find a number of people who will gladly take you up on it.

The fourth step is to begin to offer invitations. After you have talked about the weather for a few minutes while waiting to pay for your groceries, say something like, "Say, do you have time for a cup of coffee?"

Yes, you will be rejected—perhaps more often than not—but you cannot take the rejections personally. After all, these people do not really know you. As long as you extend your invitations in a friendly, nonthreatening way, you will have your share of successes. Keep in mind that countless singles (like your former, shy self) are hoping someone will approach them. By extending an invitation to have a cup of coffee, you may be doing someone a big favor.

CHAPTER FOUR

The Interpersonal Competence Questionnaire

Following are descriptions of social interactions that sometimes put people "on the spot." The purpose of this questionnaire is to find out how comfortably you could handle these situations. Use the following 5-point scale to indicate how comfortable and competent you would be in each situation. In some cases, you will have had past experiences to base your judgment on; in other cases, you may not. If you haven't had experience in a similar situation, indicate your best estimate of how you probably would respond.

---

* Reprinted with permission of Dr. Duane Buhrmester, University of California, Los Angeles, Los Angeles, California.

1 = I'm poor at this; I'd be so uncomfortable and unable to handle this situation that I'd avoid it if possible.

2 = I'm only fair at this; I'd feel very uncomfortable and would have lots of difficulty handling this situation.

3 = I'm okay at this; I'd feel somewhat uncomfortable and have some difficulty handling this situation.

4 = I'm good at this; I'd feel quite comfortable and able to handle this situation.

5 = I'm EXTREMELY good at this; I'd feel very comfortable and could handle this situation very well.

____ 1. Asking or suggesting to someone new that you get together and do something, for example, go out together.

____ 2. Telling a close companion you don't like a certain way s/he has been treating you.

____ 3. Revealing something intimate about yourself while talking with someone you're just getting to know.

____ 4. Being able to admit that you might be wrong when a disagreement with a close companion begins to build into a serious fight.

____ 5. Helping a close companion work through his/her thoughts and feelings about a major life decision.

____ 6. Finding and suggesting things to do with new people who you find interesting and attractive.

____ 7. Saying no when a new date/acquaintance asks you to do something you don't want to do.

____ 8. Confiding in a new friend/date and letting him/her see your softer, more sensitive side.

____ 9. Being able to put begrudging (resentful) feelings aside when having a fight with a close companion.

____ 10. Being able to patiently and sensitively listen to a close companion "let off steam" about outside problems s/he is going through.

____ 11. Carrying on conversations with someone new who you think you might like to get to know better.

____ 12. Turning down a request by a close companion that is unreasonable.

____ 13. Telling a close companion some things about yourself that you're ashamed of.

---

1 = I'm poor at this; 2 = I'm only fair at this; 3 = I'm okay at this;
4 = I'm good at this; 5 = I'm EXTREMELY good at this

___ 14. When having a conflict with a close companion, really listening to his/her complaints and not trying to "read" his/her mind.

___ 15. Helping a close companion get to the heart of a problem s/he is experiencing.

___ 16. Being an interesting and enjoyable person to be with when first getting to know people.

___ 17. Standing up for your rights when a close companion is neglecting you or being inconsiderate.

___ 18. Letting a new companion get to know the "real" you.

___ 19. Being able to take a close companion's perspective in a fight and really understand his/her point.

___ 20. Helping a close companion cope with family or roommate problems.

___ 21. Introducing yourself to someone you might like to get to know (or date).

___ 22. Telling a date/acquaintance that s/he is doing something that embarrasses you.

___ 23. Letting down your protective "outer shell" and trusting a close companion.

___ 24. Refraining from saying things that might cause a disagreement with a close companion to turn into a big fight.

___ 25. Being a good and sensitive listener with a close companion who is upset.

___ 26. Calling (on the phone) a new date/acquaintance to set up a time to get together and do something.

___ 27. Confronting your close companion when s/he has broken a promise.

---

1 = I'm poor at this; 2 = I'm only fair at this; 3 = I'm okay at this;
4 = I'm good at this; 5 = I'm EXTREMELY good at this

___ 28. Telling your companion about the things that secretly make you anxious or afraid.

___ 29. Being able to work through a specific problem with a close companion without resorting to global accusations (e.g., "You always do that.").

___ 30. Being able to say and do things to support a close companion when s/he is feeling put down.

___ 31. Presenting good first impressions to people you might like to become friends with (or date).

___ 32. Telling a close companion s/he has done something to hurt your feelings.

___ 33. Telling a close companion how much you appreciate and care for him/her.

___ 34. When angry with a close companion, being able to accept that s/he has a valid point of view even if you don't agree with that view.

___ 35. Being able to show genuine empathic concern when a close companion needs to talk about a problem (which may or may not interest you).

___ 36. Going to parties or gatherings where you don't know people well in order to start up new relationships.

___ 37. Telling a date/acquaintance s/he has done something that made you angry.

___ 38. Knowing how to move a conversation with a date/acquaintance beyond superficial talk in order to really get to know each other.

___ 39. Not exploding at a close companion (even when it is justified) in order to avoid a damaging fight.

___ 40. When a close companion needs help and support, being able to give advice in ways that are received well.

1 = I'm poor at this; 2 = I'm only fair at this; 3 = I'm okay at this;
    4 = I'm good at this; 5 = I'm EXTREMELY good at this

SCORING

There are five subscales to the Social Style Questionnaire. They are (1) Relationship Initiation (RI), (2) Negative Assertion (NA), (3) Self-Disclosure (SD), (4) Conflict Management (CM), and (5) Emotional Support (ES). To find your score for each subscale, simply add the values of your responses. The items that belong to each subscale are as follows:

RI	NA	SD	CM	ES
1	2	3	4	5
6	7	8	9	10
11	12	13	14	15
16	17	18	19	20
21	22	23	24	25
26	27	28	29	30
31	32	33	34	35
36	37	38	39	40

HOW DO YOU COMPARE?

RI		NA		SD		CM		ES		PERCENTILE
M	F	M	F	M	F	M	F	M	F	
32	30	31	33	32	31	32	32	37	38	85
29	27	28	30	29	28	30	30	34	36	70
26	24	26	27	26	25	28	27	32	34	50
23	21	24	24	23	22	26	24	30	32	30
20	18	21	21	20	19	24	22	27	29	15

High scores mean greater levels of the characteristic in question. If, for example, you received a percentile score of 85 on RI, it means that 85 percent of people scored lower than you did in Relationship Initiation.

For more information, see Duane Buhrmester, Wyndol Furman, Mitchell T. Wittenberg, and Harry T. Reis, "Five Domains of Interpersonal Competence in Peer Relationships," *Journal of Personality and Social Psychology* 55 (1988): 991–1008.

ABOUT THE INTERPERSONAL COMPETENCE QUESTIONNAIRE

Most of us have a tendency to point toward our partner when we try to understand why we might be having problems in a relationship. I can probably count on one hand the number of clients I have seen who came to therapy saying something like, "My relationship is not going well, and I've come to learn what I'm doing wrong." A much more common complaint is, "My relationship is not going well, and I've come to see if you can help me straighten out my partner." Although many of my clients' partners did need "straightening out," our own interpersonal competence is a powerful predictor of how satisfying and stable our relationships will be.

Psychologists have recognized this fact for some time and have constructed hundreds of tests to measure the characteristics believed necessary to form and sustain satisfying relationships. Almost without exception, these tests tried to identify a single, essential trait, but recently, Duane Buhrmester, a psychologist at UCLA, has pointed to the need to view interpersonal competence as a multifaceted phenomenon. To this end, with the help of his colleagues Wyndol Furman, Mitchell Wittenberg, and Harry Reis, he constructed the Interpersonal Competence Questionnaire to measure five requisite characteristics for the ability to form satisfying relationships.

Relationship Initiation is the first of these qualities. Scores on this scale are related to scores on the Revised Shyness Scale (see Chapter 3), and as I pointed out there, this ability is more critical for men than for women. In our society, men continue to bear much of the burden for taking the first step. It is the case, however, that women also need to attend to their scores on this scale. Only a few women are willing to be the ones to extend the first invitation, but all women must feel comfortable if they are to respond positively when a man does make that initial contact. Women with high scores on this scale are more likely to feel at ease in going to places where they might meet a potential partner, and they are likely to be more skillful in carrying their end of the conversation. In short, they are good at making it easier for men to approach them.

One interesting observation about scores on this scale is that high-scoring men are likely to have a positive feeling about their interpersonal competence regardless of their scores on the four remaining skills. Perhaps because so many people feel anxious about initiating relationships that those who are comfortable doing so tend to give their ability in this area more weight than they should.

Negative Assertion is the second dimension measured by this test. People with low scores on this scale may not experience the consequences of their inability to speak up for quite some time. Indeed, their reticence to express any feelings of anger, or even annoyance, may lead others to perceive them as "really nice guys." But over time, the anger accumulates, and unless it is handled constructively (in a way that allows conflicts to be resolved), it can undermine the relationship. Such people may never express their negative feelings directly to a partner but instead choose the strategy of withdrawal. The withdrawal may be physical—they may conclude, "I can't live with this person any more, I've got to get out." Or, the withdrawal may be psychological. They stay in the relationship physically, but they refuse to interact with their partner emotionally and perhaps sexually. The partner is often left feeling perplexed and frustrated because it is so difficult to understand what is happening.

The third dimension measured by the Interpersonal Competence Questionnaire is Self-Disclosure. Relationships are always a work in progress. And if they are to progress to the next level, the partners have to develop a sense of intimacy that comes from a willingness to share their most private and personal thoughts. Men clearly have more trouble with this than women since they seem to fear that such sharing is a sign of weakness. Indeed, I've known men who were so completely incapable of disclosing anything personal that their wives either left them or turned to an extramarital relationship in search of emotional intimacy. Feeling safe to disclose one's most private thoughts is viewed as the most valuable aspect of a romantic relationship by most people. If you have an unusually low score on this scale, the chances are good that your partner will eventually feel that you are shutting him or her out.

Conflict Management, the fourth quality measured by this test, speaks for itself. Every couple will have disagreements and arguments; the ability to resolve these in such a way so that neither partner feels belittled or threatened or concludes that he or she always ends up with the short end of the stick is critical to relationships that are to have any chance of achieving the status of long term. An essential ingredient of couples therapy is teaching the partners to fight fairly. This means trying to understand your partner's perspective, refraining from making blanket accusations and saying anything that is intended solely to be hurtful, and keeping expressions of anger under control. People who do not manage conflict well will destroy their partner's trust.

The final quality is Emotional Support, and once again, this seems to be more of a problem for men than for women. Men tend to be problem solvers. When a woman complains about her mother or something that happened at work, she, more than likely, simply wants to ventilate her feelings. She wants someone to listen to her, to acknowledge that she has good reason to feel bad, and to tell her that everything will be all right. She does not want to hear (and I learned this the hard way) "That's no problem. Why don't you . . ." I'm not sure why men and women are so different in this respect, but most women do seem to have a need to process their bad feelings. And a supportive, understanding partner helps them to get what they need.

Men, on the other hand, tend to view bad feelings as a signal that something needs to be done. If only they can find the solution, then their bad feelings will go away. While it is incumbent on men to be supportive and understanding of their partners, it is equally important for women to understand why men may seem unwilling to share their bad feelings. Men want to get rid of them as quickly as possible, and talking about them may only prolong the pain.

An especially interesting and unique element of Buhrmester's research with this test was that he and his colleagues compared their subjects' self-ratings with the ratings of the subjects made by close friends. While the correlations between the two sets of ratings were always statistically significant, they were much smaller than one might expect. For Relationship Initiation, there was a moderately close correspondence between the self and friends' ratings, but for the other four characteristics measured by this test, the correspondence was quite small. This is an important reminder that you are not always perceived the way you assume you are. You might believe you are being supportive or managing conflict well, but your best intentions matter little if your partner does not have the same view.

A useful strategy is to be explicit about your feelings when there appears to be a misunderstanding. You might say, for instance, "I'm trying to be understanding, and I'm sorry you don't feel that. Tell me what I can do to convey how much I care." As you will learn in a later section, you should never assume that your partner can read your mind.

CHAPTER FIVE

The Relationship Beliefs Inventory

The statements that follow describe ways a person might feel about a relationship with another person. Please enter the number in the blank next to each statement according to how strongly you believe that it is true or false for you. Please mark each one.

5 = I *strongly* believe that the statement is *true*.

4 = I believe that the statement is *true*.

3 = I believe that the statement is *probably true* or more true than false.

2 = I believe that the statement is *probably false* or more false than true.

1 = I believe that the statement is *false*.

0 = I *strongly* believe that the statement is *false*.

* Reprinted with permission of Dr. Norman Epstein, Center for Cognitive Therapy, University of Pennsylvania, Philadelphia, Pennsylvania.

____ 1. If your partner expresses disagreement with your ideas, s/he probably does not think highly of you.

____ 2. I do not expect my partner to sense all my moods.

____ 3. Damages done early in a relationship probably cannot be reversed.

____ 4. I get upset if I think I have not completely satisfied my partner sexually.

____ 5. Men and women have the same basic emotional needs.

____ 6. I cannot accept it when my partner disagrees with me.

____ 7. If I have to tell my partner that something is important to me, it does not mean that s/he is insensitive to me.

____ 8. My partner does not seem capable of behaving other than s/he does.

____ 9. If I'm not in the mood for sex when my partner is, I don't get upset about it.

____ 10. Misunderstandings between partners generally are due to inborn differences in psychological makeups of men and women.

____ 11. I take it as a personal insult when my partner disagrees with an important idea of mine.

____ 12. I get very upset if my partner does not recognize how I am feeling and I have to tell him/her.

____ 13. A partner can learn to become more responsive to his/her partner's needs.

____ 14. A good sexual partner can get himself/herself aroused for sex whenever necessary.

____ 15. Men and women probably will never understand the opposite sex very well.

5 = Strongly true; 4 = True; 3 = Probably true;
2 = Probably false; 1 = False; 0 = Strongly false

___ 16. I like it when my partner presents views different from mine.

___ 17. People who have a close relationship can sense each other's needs as if they could read each other's minds.

___ 18. Just because my partner has acted in ways that upset me does not mean that s/he will do so in the future.

___ 19. If I cannot perform well sexually whenever my partner is in the mood, I would consider that I have a problem.

___ 20. Men and women need the same basic things out of a relationship.

___ 21. I get very upset when my partner and I cannot see things the same way.

___ 22. It is important to me for my partner to anticipate my needs by sensing changes in my moods.

___ 23. A partner who hurts you badly once probably will hurt you again.

___ 24. I can feel okay about my lovemaking even if my partner does not achieve orgasm.

___ 25. Biological differences between men and women are not major causes of couples' problems.

___ 26. I cannot tolerate it when my partner argues with me.

___ 27. A partner should know what you are thinking or feeling without you having to tell him/her.

___ 28. If my partner wants to change, I believe that s/he can do it.

___ 29. If my sexual partner does not get satisfied completely, it does not mean that I have failed.

___ 30. One of the major causes of marital problems is that men and women have different emotional needs.

5 = Strongly true; 4 = True; 3 = Probably true;
2 = Probably false; 1 = False; 0 = Strongly false

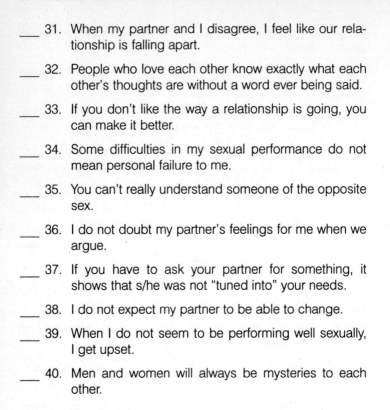

___ 31. When my partner and I disagree, I feel like our relationship is falling apart.

___ 32. People who love each other know exactly what each other's thoughts are without a word ever being said.

___ 33. If you don't like the way a relationship is going, you can make it better.

___ 34. Some difficulties in my sexual performance do not mean personal failure to me.

___ 35. You can't really understand someone of the opposite sex.

___ 36. I do not doubt my partner's feelings for me when we argue.

___ 37. If you have to ask your partner for something, it shows that s/he was not "tuned into" your needs.

___ 38. I do not expect my partner to be able to change.

___ 39. When I do not seem to be performing well sexually, I get upset.

___ 40. Men and women will always be mysteries to each other.

SCORING

There are five subscales to the Relationship Beliefs Inventory. They are (1) Disagreement Is Destructive (DD), (2) Mindreading Is Expected (ME), (3) Partners Cannot Change (PCC), (4) Sexual Perfectionism (SP), and (5) the Sexes Are Different (SD). To find your score for each subscale, simply add the values of your responses after you have reversed the scoring for the

5 = Strongly true; 4 = True; 3 = Probably true;
2 = Probably false; 1 = False; 0 = Strongly false

indicated items. The items that belong to each subscale are as follows:

DD	ME	PCC	SP	SD
1	2*	3	4	5*
6	7*	8	9*	10
11	12	13*	14	15
16*	17	18*	19	20*
21	22	23	24*	25*
26	27	28*	29*	30
31	32	33*	34*	35
36*	37	38	39	40

* The items marked with an asterisk should be reverse scored (i.e., 0 = 5, 1 = 4, 2 = 3, 3 = 2, 4 = 1, and 5 = 0).

How Do You Compare?

DD	ME	PCC	SP	SD	PERCENTILE
18	24	20	21	23	85
15	21	18	19	20	70
12	19	15	16	17	50
9	17	12	13	14	30
6	14	10	11	11	15

High scores indicate higher levels of the characteristic in question. If, for instance, you received a percentile score of 15 on ME, it means that 15 percent of people have a lower level of belief than you do that Mindreading Is Expected.

For more information, see Roy J. Eidelson and Norman Epstein, "Cognition and Relationship Maladjustment: Development of a Measure of Dysfunctional Relationship Beliefs," *Journal of Consulting and Clinical Psychology* 5 (1982): 715–720.

ABOUT THE RELATIONSHIP BELIEF INVENTORY

This test was something of a shock to me. Like most people, I pride myself on being a rational, logical person. And like most people, I believe I have what it takes to have a stable, satisfying relationship. After all, I have been married to the same woman for nearly thirty years. So, imagine my surprise when I received above-average scores on three of the five scales on the Relationship Belief Inventory.

This test, developed by psychologists Roy Eidelson and Norman Epstein, was created to serve as a tool for both researchers and practitioners who specialize in relationships. Over the past fifteen years or so, a growing body of scientific evidence has established that men's and women's beliefs about the nature of relationships play an important role in the quality of their own relationships. Not only are certain beliefs associated with lower levels of satisfaction with one's relationship, but these beliefs, called dysfunctional relationship beliefs, can destroy one's motivation to try to make things better. Men and women who hold dysfunctional relationship beliefs may even view therapy as pointless; they simply do not believe it can make any difference. According to Eidelson and Epstein, I have a few dysfunctional relationship beliefs of my own.

The first scale on which I received an above-average score (I refuse to say how much above average) is the Sexes Are Different scale. People who believe that men and women are dramatically different in their personalities and what they want from a relationship are thought to respond to their partners in terms of stereotypes rather than reality. This in turn makes them less sensitive to their partners' characteristics and needs. Furthermore, a belief that men and women are dramatically different may lead to the conclusion that there is no point in trying to resolve conflicts: If they are so different, men and women will never be able to see eye to eye.

Okay, I agree with all that. I believe that the differences among men and among women are much greater than the differences between the average man and the average woman, so one should always react to one's partner on the basis of his or her personality rather than stereotypes. But the reality (at least as I see it) is that there are rather consistent differences between the sexes that can cause problems for couples who are not sensitive to them.

As one example, men and women view their relationships in slightly different ways. Most men value them highly but consider them to be just one piece of the puzzle. If things are not going well at home, they can pour their energies into their jobs or their hobbies. And as long as there is no open conflict and hostility between them and their partners, they can be relatively content. Women, on the other hand, are likely to view their relationships as the centerpieces of their lives. Of the hundreds of couples I've seen in therapy over the years, I can recall only one woman who derived most of her satisfaction from her work and was willing to tolerate a cool, distant relationship with her husband. For women, if things are not going well at home, they tend to conclude that their lives are not going well.

I also scored higher than average on the Disagreement Is Destructive scale. The items on this scale were difficult for me to respond to because Meredith, my wife, tends to agree with my views a high percentage of the time—as I do with hers. For me, one of the most valuable elements of my marriage is having someone in my life whom I know I can count on to be on my side and to be supportive of my occasional flights of fancy. If Meredith were to tell me regularly that my ideas were nonsense or that she could not go along with some plan I had hatched, I don't think I would be as happy in my marriage as I am. Certainly all couples will disagree at times, and certainly successful couples must treat such differences with respect, but I believe that couples who agree more often than not are likely to be happier with their relationships.

My third above-average score was on the Partners Cannot Change scale. Here, I admit to being somewhat cynical. I believe that people can make small, subtle changes, but I also believe the truism that the best predictor of future behavior is past behavior. Although Meredith and I have come to accept each other's frailties, we have the same complaints about each other today that we had twenty-five years ago. On the more serious side, I've seen countless situations in therapy where one partner exhibited chronic anger, substance abuse, infidelity, and the like and very little evidence that such people change their ways. Anything is possible, but my experience suggests that more heartbreak results from people refusing to give up on the hope that their partner will change than from their believing that their partner cannot change.

The belief measured by the fourth scale, Mindreading Is Expected, may get some couples in trouble because women are usually better at nonverbal communication than are men. A woman is likely to be sensitive and responsive to her partner's moods and feelings without his having to verbalize them. A man gets himself into trouble because his partner expects the same sensitivity and responsiveness in return. Unfortunately, men are not very good at this. I've heard countless men paraphrase the title of this scale: "She expects me to read her mind." Women, on the other hand, complain that they should not be put in the position of having to ask for support, affection, understanding—whatever they may need at the moment. They believe that their partners "should just know" when they need these things. I believe wise men will try to be more sensitive to the moods and feelings of the women in their lives, and wise women will be more explicit as to what they would like from their partners.

The name of the final scale, Sexual Perfectionism, says it all. People with high scores on this scale set such high standards for their own sexual performance and that of their partners that they are bound to be disappointed. Yes, it would be nice if your partner was always in the mood when you were. And your partner would think it equally nice if you were always in the mood when he or she was. But over the course of a long-term relationship, there are likely to be as many sexual encounters in which one partner is acting magnanimously as there are encounters desired equally by both partners. Satisfied couples are those who are skilled in the art of compromise.

Eidelson and Epstein provided evidence that scores on their test, especially the Disagreement Is Destructive scale, were related to overall marital adjustment. People with higher scores were less satisfied with their relationships. Among men and women seeking therapy for their marital problems, those with high scores tended to have less hope that their relationships could improve, were more likely to view divorce or separation as the most desirable goal, and expressed a preference for individual therapy rather than couples therapy.

A curious result—and one that makes me feel better about the prospects of my marriage lasting—was the finding that for average couples, scores on the Partners Cannot Change scale did not bear any relationship to satisfaction with the relationship. For couples who were seeking marital therapy, however, scores on this scale were strongly related to dissatisfaction with the relationship. As Eidelson and Epstein pointed out, this apparent discrepancy may be explained by examining the association between beliefs and behaviors. To illustrate, my belief that partners do not change much may not be an impediment in my marriage because the things Meredith does to annoy me are mostly rather trivial. I'm not about to call it quits even though I've given up trying to get her to put the cap back on the toothpaste. On the other hand, for the people who live with physically abusive or alcoholic partners, a belief that partners cannot change will have a much greater effect on their level of satisfaction.

If you had several scores on the Relationship Belief Inventory at the 85th percentile or higher, it does not, by itself, mean that your relationship is in trouble. Like me, you may have a few dysfunctional relationship beliefs about rather trivial issues. If, however, you are experiencing distress about your relationship, high scores on these scales may provide a clue as to where you can start in your attempt to make your relationship work. As my father used to advise me, you need to try to develop a better attitude.

CHAPTER SIX

The Locus of Control of Interpersonal Relationships Questionnaire

For each item, choose the statement (a or b) that you *most agree with*, and put a check mark next to that item. Please answer every item.

---

* Reprinted with permission of Dr. Philip Lewis, Auburn University, Auburn, Alabama.

1. ___   (a) Heredity plays a major role in determining one's personality.

   ___   (b) It is one's experiences in life that determine what one is like.

2. ___   (a) In the long run, people get the respect they deserve from others.

   ___   (b) Unfortunately, an individual's worth often passes unrecognized no matter how hard he or she tries.

3. ___   (a) Without the right breaks, one cannot be an effective leader.

   ___   (b) Capable people who fail to become leaders have not taken advantage of their opportunities.

4. ___   (a) People who can't get others to like them don't understand how to get along with others.

   ___   (b) No matter how hard you try, some people just don't like you.

5. ___   (a) It is hard to know whether or not a person really likes you

   ___   (b) How many friends you have depends upon how nice a person you are.

6. ___   (a) People are lonely because they don't try to be friendly.

   ___   (b) There's not much use in trying to please people; if they like you, they like you.

7. ___   (a) Who gets to be boss often depends on who was lucky enough to be in the right place first.

   ___   (b) Getting people to do the right thing depends upon ability; luck has little or nothing to do with it.

8. ___   (a) Children get into trouble because their parents push them too much.

   ___   (b) The trouble with most children nowadays is that their parents are too easy with them.

9. ___ (a) Even if a person rejects you at first, by trying hard enough you can usually win him or her over.

___ (b) Some people simply won't accept you as you are, and it doesn't help to worry about it.

10. ___ (a) Certain people never seem to be able to follow instructions.

___ (b) How well people follow instructions depends upon how well you explain and clarify what is expected.

11. ___ (a) When I have to, I can find a way to get almost anyone's attention.

___ (b) Some people are so wrapped up in their own affairs that they never pay me any attention.

12. ___ (a) When I really care about something, I can usually get everybody to see things my way.

___ (b) Some narrow-minded people are just not influenced by anything I say or do.

13. ___ (a) Although they may be nice and easy to get along with, some people just aren't very interesting.

___ (b) If people get to know one another, they can almost always find something interesting in each other.

14. ___ (a) If a person shows enough patience, he or she can win the trust of almost anybody.

___ (b) There are some people who are so suspicious that they seldom let anyone get close to them.

15. ___ (a) People should learn to accept others the way they are, because it usually doesn't do any good to try to change another person.

___ (b) People who really care can often stimulate important changes in other people.

16. ___ (a) There are certain people who are just no good.

___ (b) There is some good in everybody.

17. ___ (a) How you act determines how people will react to you.

___ (b) Who you are is sometimes more important than what you do in determining the way people treat you.

18. ___ (a) Whether people take my advice is usually dependent upon whether they are willing to accept help from others.

___ (b) When I make up my mind, I can get most people to follow my advice.

19. ___ (a) When people get angry, you can usually talk them through it if you stay calm yourself.

___ (b) When people get angry, it is best to leave them alone until they calm down.

20. ___ (a) Some people are so serious minded, it's almost impossible to get them to laugh.

___ (b) You can get anybody to laugh if you approach them in the right way.

21. ___ (a) Some people could care less about getting to know me.

___ (b) When I care to, I can have a real impact on most people.

22. ___ (a) If you really listen, you can communicate with most anybody.

___ (b) Some people are so different from you that you will never be able to communicate with them.

23. ___ (a) One should always be willing to admit mistakes.

___ (b) It is usually best to cover up one's mistakes.

24. ___ (a) It is not unusual to find people with entirely different backgrounds constantly disagreeing.

___ (b) Regardless of the differences in their experiences, people can learn to get along well with each other.

25. ___ (a) I can make almost anyone understand who I am and what I believe.

___ (b) Many people would have a hard time really understanding me.

26. ___ (a) There are some people that I just don't like, and it's usually best for all of us if I keep myself from getting involved with them.

___ (b) Whether or not I like someone usually depends upon how well I get to know them.

27. ___ (a) I find that leading others isn't hard if I always set the example.

___ (b) No matter what I do to try to change them, some people will always do things their own way.

28. ___ (a) There is too much emphasis on athletics in high school.

___ (b) Team sports are an excellent way to build character.

Scoring

The following are filler items and are not counted in the final score: 1, 8, 16, 23, and 28. To calculate your total score, give yourself one point for each of your responses that match those listed.

2. B	9. B	15. A	22. B
3. A	10. A	17. B	24. A
4. B	11. B	18. A	25. B
5. A	12. B	19. B	26. A
6. B	13. A	20. A	27. B
7. A	14. B	21. A	

How Do You Compare?

Score	Percentile
14	85
12	70
10	50
8	30
6	15

High scores indicate a greater External Locus of Control. If, for example, you scored at the 85th percentile, it means that 85 percent of people have a more Internal Locus of Control than do you.

For more information, see Philip Lewis, Thomas Cheney, and A. Stephen Dawes, "Locus of Control of Interpersonal Relationships Questionnaire," *Psychological Reports* 41 (1977): 507–510.

About the Locus of Control of Interpersonal Relationships Questionnaire

If your relationships have not been as satisfying as you would like, how do you explain this to yourself? Do you believe you have been the victim of bad luck? Perhaps you have not yet met the right person? Or could it be possible that there is something about you that could be getting in your way?

The Locus of Control of Interpersonal Relationships Questionnaire will provide an indication of what you believe the answer is to this question. Developed by psychologists Philip Lewis, Thomas Cheney, and A. Stephen Dawes, this test is intended to predict how people will behave in social situations. Their test is a refinement of a general Locus of Control Scale developed by the eminent psychologist Julian Rotter. Rotter observed that while some people, those with an External Locus of Control, seemed to believe that they were hapless victims of fate, others took an active role in influencing their futures. These people, said to have an Internal Locus of Control, believed that their efforts would make a difference in what would happen to them. Lewis and his colleagues reasoned that Rotter's theory could be extended to differences among people in how they handled interpersonal problems. Those with an External Locus of Control of Interpersonal Relationships believe there is little they can do to influence the kinds of relationships they have with others. This view holds that people are pretty much what they are, and there is little you can do about it. Those with an Internal Locus of Control of Interpersonal Relationships recognize that the ways in which they interact with others have an impact on how they will be received and treated in return.

I remember vividly one former client—I'll call him Larry—who had an extreme External Locus of Control. He came to therapy depressed because his wife, Sandy, told him that she wanted a divorce. Larry had a responsible position with a major corporation, and Sandy had her own small business. But despite their sizable income, Larry's spending habits were such that they were not able to meet the minimum monthly payments on their credit cards. Larry, who had gained 100 pounds since his marriage, had a quick temper, and Sandy, who was quite assertive herself, was still no match for him when they had one of their numerous disagreements. He always walked away the winner.

At my behest, Sandy agreed to accompany Larry to therapy for one session. Her position was straightforward: "Larry refuses either to stop spending so much money or to get a better job to help pay some of the bills. His temper is so bad that I've given up trying to express my opinion about anything. It just isn't worth it. On top of his being impossible to get along with, he has let himself go to the point where I find him repulsive. I can't stand to have him touch me, much less make love to me."

After Sandy finished her litany of complaints, I turned to Larry for his response. "I can't understand why she won't accept me for what I am" was his only defense.

I had several more sessions with Larry, who was incapable of seeing his role in his marital problems (or perhaps I was incapable of helping him to see it). He admitted he sometimes spent too much money. But he felt that because his family couldn't afford nice things while he was growing up, it was important to him to have them as an adult. And yes, he did have quite a temper, but Sandy knew that that was just the way he was and that he really loved her despite all the harsh things he said to her when he was angry. And perhaps he should try to control his eating and begin exercising, but how could Sandy be so superficial to react so strongly to a little extra weight? Larry truly believed that the solution to his marital problems was for Sandy to learn to accept him for the lovable person he was deep inside. There was nothing he could do, or should be expected to do, to improve their relationship.

While Larry was an extreme case, it is usually difficult to convince people with an External Locus of Control of Relationships that there might be a better way of thinking about their own situations. In part, this difficulty is understandable because many of their beliefs do have a large grain of truth to them. The alternative indicating externality for Item 6, for instance, reads, "There's not much use in trying too hard to please people. If they like you, they like you." That certainly is true in many cases. I know there are people who will never like me regardless of how hard I tried to ingratiate myself. But on the other hand, people who place too much credence in this statement might not make even a minimal effort to be friendly and interested when meeting new people.

One observation made by a number of psychologists over the past few decades is that our perceptions may be more important than reality. And the reality is that all of the alternatives indicating externality on this test are accurate for some people we might meet, under some circumstances. But if we perceive that our own efforts to be friendly and accepting and that our own interpersonal skills make a difference in the kinds of relationships we are able to form, we are likely to make an effort to be the best partner we can be. Although there are never any guarantees, this effort is likely to pay rich dividends.

I've heard many so-called experts say something similar to what Larry said about his wife—that love is purest and most noble when it is unconditional. My view is that unconditional love between romantic partners never exists, nor should it ever exist. Yes, I would agree that a love with any substance to it will allow one to overlook certain flaws in a partner. Meredith certainly has demonstrated her capacity to love by staying with me despite my numerous imperfections. But on the other hand, there have to be limits as to what we can be expected to overlook. I would never, for instance, continue to love a partner who abused our children. And I could not blame Sandy for wanting to leave a husband who did not shoulder his share of the relationship's responsibilities or who was continually vituperative and angry. Everyone who wants a stable and satisfying relationship must strive to be the best partner possible.

If you received a high score on the Locus of Control of Interpersonal Relationships Questionnaire and if you have been disappointed with your past relationships, you may profit from taking a close look at yourself. The first five tests in Part I of this book may be a good place to start. Are you a trusting partner? Do you provide emotional support for your partner? Do you manage conflict effectively? These are just a few of the questions you should ask yourself. Everyone can have one, maybe two, unhappy relationships solely as a result of bad luck. But if you have had more than your share, the odds are good that more than simple bad luck is at work.

PART II

Falling in Love

After taking the tests in Part II, you will know how you experience love, what you believe about love, and how love influences your perceptions and behavior. The following tests are included in Part II:

CHAPTER SEVEN

The Romantic Symptoms Questionnaire

Following is a list of feelings that may be elicited by the thought of your romantic partner. Respond with the word *true* for those that you feel and the word *false* for those that you do not feel. Respond in terms of your current (right now) feelings, not in terms of your general feelings.

* Reprinted with permission of Dr. Eugene W. Mathes, Western Illinois University, Macomb, Illinois.

___   1. As if each day is special

___   2. That life is worthwhile

___   3. Happy about everything

___   4. As if I were swinging very high

___   5. That he or she is perfect

___   6. Positive toward everyone

___   7. High

___   8. Energetic

___   9. In tune with my body

___ 10. Wow!

___ 11. Delirious

___ 12. Like counting the minutes until I see her or him

___ 13. As if we lived in our own special world

___ 14. Able to accomplish any goal

___ 15. Spontaneous

___ 16. Extreme joy

___ 17. That she or he is the most beautiful person in the world

___ 18. Totally involved with him or her

___ 19. Oneness and harmony with her or him

___ 20. In love with everything

___ 21. A tingling in my spine

___ 22. Breathless

___ 23. Longing for her or him

___ 24. Tingly

___ 25. Light

___ 26. Carefree

___ 27. Like jumping up and down

___ 28. As if I didn't have a care in the world

___ 29. Generous

___ 30. Playful

___ 31. Fulfilled

___ 32. Radiating

___ 33. Beaming

___ 34. Accepting

___ 35. Preoccupied with thoughts of her or him

___ 36. Good will toward the world

___ 37. Complete

___ 38. Thrills of anticipation

___ 39. Off in the clouds

___ 40. Constant euphoria

___ 41. Floating

___ 42. A kind of pressure or burning in my genitals

___ 43. Able to conquer all

___ 44. Full

___ 45. Overwhelmed by my feelings

___ 46. Like acting crazy

___ 47. As if the whole world were coming up roses

___ 48. Light and airy

___ 49. Purposeful

___ 50. An increased heartbeat

___ 51. Flushed

___ 52. Unrestrained

___ 53. Oneness

___ 54. Loyalty

___ 55. Self-actualizing

___ 56. Exuberance

___ 57. Ecstasy

___ 58. Vigorous

___ 59. Bursting with happiness

___ 60. Whole

___ 61. Like a blind person who has suddenly gained his or her sight

___ 62. That everything is good

___ 63. An increased metabolism

___ 64. Fantastic

___ 65. Dazed

___ 66. Like singing

___ 67. As if a rainbow were shining just for me

___ 68. Like blossoming

___ 69. Awake

___ 70. Sunny

___ 71. All aglow

___ 72. Heightened sensory awareness

___ 73. Like exploding

___ 74. About to burst with happiness

___ 75. A big rush inside me

___ 76. Like screaming for joy

SCORING

To calculate your score, add up the number of items you marked as *true*.

HOW DO YOU COMPARE?

MEN	WOMEN	PERCENTILE
58	63	85
49	52	70
40	46	50
31	38	30
22	29	15

High scores indicate more romantic symptoms.

For more information, see Eugene W. Mathes, "Mystical Experiences, Romantic Love, and Hypnotic Susceptibility," *Psychological Reports* 50 (1982): 701–702.

ABOUT THE ROMANTIC LOVE SYMPTOMS CHECKLIST

Romantic love can be an intense emotional experience. When we are in love, we feel on top of the world, we have the sense we are walking on air, we believe the world is a wonderful place—the list could go on and on. Indeed, psychologist Eugene Mathes expanded this list greatly and developed a scale that surveys seventy-six symptoms of romantic love. As you could see when you converted your score on this test to a percentile score, half of all men and women indicated they experienced at least forty of these symptoms, and fully 15 percent of men and women experienced at least fifty-seven of the seventy-six symptoms. And about 2 percent of men and women experienced seventy-four of seventy-six symptoms. Wow!

Mathes's love test is unique in that it is the only one I've seen that focuses only on the emotional experience of romantic love. As you will see in the sections that follow, most similar tests treat love as a multidimensional experience. That is, the authors view love as comprised of not only emotions but also certain attitudes and beliefs. Although most experts would agree that it is more accurate to view love as a complex state, Mathes's test is useful because emotions play such a critical role in the experience of romantic love.

Psychologist Dorothy Tennov has written extensively about the emotional aspects of romantic love. She has argued that the emotional component is what distinguishes loving from liking. Although we may feel a certain affection for a friend, we are unlikely to feel nervous and jittery in anticipation of meeting with a friend as compared with a lover. And while we may feel a sense of gratification at having a really good friend, when we are in love, we are likely to feel that we can conquer the world, that we are in harmony with mother nature herself.

Tennov interviewed nearly one thousand men and women about their romantic love experiences and found that they described their bodily sensations with a surprising consistency. People in love talked about a sense of lightness, a feeling that they were walking on air. The reports were so consistent that Tennov concluded there may be a specific physiological response that accounts for the emotion of love. Subsequently, other researchers have identified a naturally occurring chemical in the body (as discussed earlier), phenylethylamine (PEA, for short), that might be responsible for the symptoms of love. PEA produces high energy levels and a sense of euphoria and elation. Love may be an amphetamine high.

On the other side of the coin, she concluded that people who have lost their true love may also experience a specific physiological response. Such men and women consistently talked about a painful feeling of heaviness in their midsection. The expression *broken heart* may very well reflect an area of the body where physiological activity causes people to experience the pain of an unrequited love.

Perhaps the most startling discovery by Tennov was that not everyone experiences the emotions associated with being in love. She learned this while discussing her research with a colleague. Tennov was telling her friend about the bodily sensations her subjects reported and some of the silly, perhaps slightly crazy things they did while they were trying to win the heart of the person with whom they were in love. "Those people are crazy!" exclaimed Tennov's colleague. Tennov was surprised by the response because she apparently had done some silly things herself in the name of love. She viewed her subjects as being completely normal. After further questioning, Tennov learned that her colleague, although happily married for many years, had never experienced the pounding heart, the butterflies in the stomach, or any of the symptoms most of us have found so exhilarating.

Tennov kept this new perspective in mind when interviewing the remainder of her subjects and concluded that from 15 to 20 percent of the population simply do not experience the emotional side of love. Some of these people believed they were missing something important. They had heard their friends talk about the ecstasy of being in love, and they felt frustrated that they could not find a partner who inspired such feelings. Others from this group who had never experienced the emotions of romantic love felt fortunate.

They pointed to the irrational behavior of their friends who were in love and the pain and suffering their friends experienced when a relationship soured. Many of these men and women deemed themselves lucky that they were not prone to such nonsense. It is intriguing to speculate that these people may not necessarily be as rational and smart as they think they are. They may simply have deficient PEA levels.

Although the emotional high that results from being in love can be a wonderful experience, it can have a downside. The elation and ecstasy associated with love can cause people to see their partners in an idealized way; that is, lovers tend to wear rose-colored glasses. They simply cannot see their lovers' faults, and if they do catch a glimmering of them, they are quick to explain them away.

Donna was guilty of this. In her words, "I was madly in love with Rob, and I thought he was perfect in every way. Two months after our first date he asked me to marry him, and I didn't hesitate. I couldn't believe how lucky I was.

"About three months later, I couldn't help but admit that his drinking made me feel uncomfortable. Earlier in our relationship we often went out to clubs or to parties, and I didn't pay much attention to how much he drank—even though I had to drive home much of the time. But when we started to spend more time at home, it bothered me that he could go through a couple of six packs while watching a movie on television. When I would say something about it, he would make a joke about enjoying his last months of freedom, and I would forget about it.

"Looking back, I realize I had plenty of warning signals. One night we were going to meet my parents for dinner, and when he picked me up, I could tell he had had a lot to drink. I was angry about it because I knew how my parents would react. When I told him how I felt, he just exploded. He screamed that I wasn't his mother and that I had better not try to control him. Later, he apologized and told me the stress of the wedding was getting to him. I was sure he would settle down after we were married.

"His drinking only got worse. He was pretty good on our honeymoon, but once we got settled into our apartment, he passed out almost every night. Within a year, I couldn't stand for him to touch me, and I could barely stand the sight of him. I don't know how I could have been so blind."

While Donna's rose-colored glasses may have had an unusually dark tint, she is by no means alone. For most people, the pure joy of being in love makes it difficult to evaluate whether their lovers are the types of persons whose company they will continue to enjoy several years down the road when the intensity of their feelings begins to fade.

So, if you had an unusually high score on the Romantic Love Symptom Questionnaire, revel in your sensations. You are feeling emotions that some people will never experience. But on the other hand, be careful. Try not to allow your emotions to obscure your objectivity. Remember, this is the person you will be waking up next to long after your heart has stopped pounding from the mere anticipation of being with him or her.

CHAPTER EIGHT

The Romantic Potential Questionnaire

The following statements describe how you feel about a person of the opposite sex with whom you have some sort of relationship. For example, consider this statement: You respect him (her). Rate this statement, and all the others, on a scale from 0 to 10. (You may use any number from 0 to 10 to express how strongly you feel.)

 0 = You do not feel that way at all at the present time.
 5 = You feel that way moderately.
10 = You feel that way strongly.

* Reprinted with the permission of Alvin Pam, Albert Einstein College of Medicine, New York, New York.

___ 1. You take his (her) suggestions seriously.

___ 2. You feel privileged to know him (her).

___ 3. You think he (she) copes well with his (her) own problems.

___ 4. He (she) has unusual competence or skills.

___ 5. He (she) has better judgment than the average person.

___ 6. He (she) is more intelligent than the average person.

___ 7. He (she) is more ethical than the average person.

___ 8. You respect him (her).

___ 9. You and he (she) get along well as a couple.

___ 10. You like sharing experiences with him (her).

___ 11. He (she) does not say or do things that embarrass you.

___ 12. He (she) can accept you as you really are.

___ 13. There are times when you seem to know what each wants without words.

___ 14. You are confident he (she) will stand by you through difficult times.

___ 15. You feel he (she) understands you.

___ 16. You and he (she) can work it out when you have a difference of opinion.

___ 17. You like giving gifts to him (her).

___ 18. You go out of your way to do things he (she) will enjoy.

___ 19. You enjoy taking care of him (her).

___ 20. You are willing to make sacrifices for him (her).

---

0 = You do not feel that way at all at the present time;
5 = You feel that way moderately; 10 = You feel that way strongly

___ 21. You get very angry if someone hurts him (her).

___ 22. You suffer when he (she) suffers.

___ 23. You are willing to suffer to prevent him (her) from suffering.

___ 24. You would be willing to die for him (her).

___ 25. You think he (she) is better looking than average.

___ 26. You like to show him (her) off.

___ 27. You spontaneously want to express affection toward him (her).

___ 28. He (she) is sexually attractive to you.

___ 29. You like being touched by him (her).

___ 30. You enjoy caressing him (her).

___ 31. You want to embrace him (her).

___ 32. You are sexually excited by him (her).

___ 33. It is important to be noticed by him (her).

___ 34. It is important to be praised by him (her).

___ 35. You feel more secure when you are with him (her).

___ 36. You feel good when he (she) is sensitive to your moods and feelings.

___ 37. You would be jealous if he (she) became involved with someone else.

___ 38. He (she) is necessary for your present personal happiness.

___ 39. He (she) is necessary for the fulfillment of your needs.

___ 40. You would suffer if you lost him (her).

---

0 = You do not feel that way at all at the present time;
5 = You feel that way moderately; 10 = You feel that way strongly

SCORING

There are five subscales to the Romantic Potential Questionnaire. They are (1) Respect (R), (2) Congeniality (C), (3) Altruism (Al), (4) Physical Attraction (PA), and (5) Attachment (At). To find your score on each subscale, sum your responses to each item on the relevant subscale. The items belonging to each subscale are as follows:

Respect	Items 1–8
Congeniality	Items 9–16
Altruism	Items 17–24
Physical Attraction	Items 25–32
Attachment	Items 33–40

HOW DO YOU COMPARE?

R	C	AL	PA	AT	TOTAL	PERCENTILE
62	66	58	69	62	302	85
56	60	52	60	55	275	70
50	54	46	51	47	248	50
44	48	40	42	39	221	30
38	42	34	33	32	194	15

High scores indicate higher levels of the characteristic in question. If, for example, your R score was at the 70th percentile, it means that you have more respect for your partner than 70 percent of people have for theirs.

For more information, see Alvin Pam, Robert Plutchik, and Hope R. Conte, Love, A Psychometric Approach. *Psychological Reports* 37 (1975): 83–88.

ABOUT THE ROMANTIC POTENTIAL QUESTIONNAIRE

Suppose that you have met someone who seems to have potential as a romantic partner. You like this person, enjoy your time together, and begin to wonder if these feelings could blossom into love. Is there any way to know if this is a realistic possibility?

The Romantic Potential Questionnaire, developed by psychologists Alvin Pam, Robert Plutchik, and Hope Conte, may be just what you are looking for. In the mid-1970s, these researchers noted that for the most part, psychologists had ignored love. Because this is an emotion that plays such a prominent role in our loves, they felt something should be done about this oversight, and consequently, they developed one of the first psychological tests that focused on the experience of love. Borrowing from the writings of the French novelist Stendhal, the Spanish philosopher Ortega y Gasset, and the contemporary social critic Dennis de Rougemont, these psychologists set out to devise an instrument that captured the essence of this complex emotion. The result was a test with five subscales: Respect, Congeniality, Altruism, Physical Attraction, and Attachment. These, of course, are the five dimensions on which you received scores for the Romantic Potential Questionnaire.

To provide evidence for the validity of their test, the authors administered it to three groups of people: a group of men and women who reported they were in love, a group who were dating someone (the norms provided here were based on this group), and a group who said they were friends with someone of the opposite sex. As the psychologists expected, the men and women who were in love had the highest scores of the three groups on all five dimensions.

There were, however, some interesting results when those in love were compared with the other two groups. For instance, men and women reported greater Respect for their opposite sex friends than they did for their dating partners. But while dating partners were afforded less Respect than friends, they inspired more Physical Attraction. Dating partners and friends received similar scores on the other three dimensions. It is curious that apparently we are willing to date people for whom we have less Respect than we have for our friends. Perhaps this illustrates the power of Physical Attraction.

It was encouraging to note that the men and women in love had high scores on all the dimensions when describing their feelings for their partners. This is not always the case. A common problem experienced by people in love is that they may not especially like their lovers. Psychologists Ellen Hatfield and Elaine Walster, who have given countless talks about love to college students and community groups, have said that the question they are asked more than any other is, Can you love someone and hate him at the same time? Their answer is, Yes, it is entirely possible.

Many people experience strong feelings of Physical Attraction and Attachment, perhaps even altruism, for their partners and conclude that they are hopelessly in love. But these same people regularly experience intense anger at their partners and avoid introducing them to family and friends because they are embarrassed by them. In other words, despite their protestations of having found their one and only, they do not have strong feelings of Respect or Congeniality for their partners.

Perhaps the strong feelings of Physical Attraction and Attachment would be enough to sustain a relationship except for one very important problem: These feelings tend to fade with time. So, many people have made lifelong commitments to partners they were hopelessly in love with only to discover a few years later that they couldn't stand the sight of them.

Pam, Plutchik, and Conte found that on average, their men and women in love had extremely strong feelings of Respect and Congeniality for their partners, and this is a testament to the good sense that most people have most of the time. Nonetheless, there are probably few people who have not had the experience of falling in love with the wrong person. This Romantic Potential Scale should provide you with a sense of whether this has happened to you.

If you have scores that are well above the 50th percentile for Physical Attraction and Attachment, and possibly Altruism, but well below the 50th percentile for Respect and Congeniality, you might want to think long and hard before making a commitment. Remember, three years from now the chemistry between you and your lover will not be as strong as it is today, and you will have to ask yourself if this is the sort of person you admire, the sort of person you can enjoy spending the rest of your life with. You want to find a romantic partner whom you can rate as high on the Respect and Congeniality scales as you would any of your friends.

What should you do if you are in love with someone for whom you have low feelings of Respect and

Congeniality? Barbara found herself in this position, and she found a solution that worked for her. "I fell in love with Don when I was a junior in high school. We were married two years later, and within another year, I realized what a mistake I had made. He had no ambition, and his idea of a good time was to leave me at home while he went out drinking with his friends.

"I had a few relationships after I divorced Don, but nothing special until I was nearly thirty years old. I knew I was hopelessly in love with Gil within a month of meeting him. He said he felt the same way about me and asked me to marry him. But I was scared to death of making another mistake. I couldn't see Don clearly when I was consumed with love, and I was afraid I wasn't seeing Gil clearly either.

"Finally, I agreed to move in with him, but I told him I wasn't making any promises. It was about a year and a half later that I knew I was ready to make a commitment. We had an argument, and we didn't speak to each other for several hours. Finally, he came into the bedroom and said we should try to talk about it. It was then that I realized what a mature, sensible person he was. At that moment, I was confident that I was seeing him clearly, and I knew I wanted to marry him. I proposed on the spot, and he accepted, after observing it was one hell of a strategy for ending an argument. So I guess you could say I decided to marry Gil when my feelings of 'being in love' began to fade. It may seem like a strange way to do things, but it worked out for me. I've never regretted my decision in the twelve years we've been married."

Barbara was smart enough to realize her feelings of passion made it difficult for her to objectively evaluate her relationship with Gil. Not everyone sees their romantic partner with the same rose-colored glasses as Barbara did, but if you have any suspicion that you fall into the same category, you would be well advised to be brutally honest with yourself when you complete the Romantic Potential Questionnaire. You should never use the results of a psychological test as the sole basis for making a decision, but if you do have low scores on Respect and Congeniality, you should consider carefully the implications of making a commitment to a person you feel this way about.

CHAPTER NINE

The Romantic Beliefs Scale

Please rate the degree to which you agree with each of the following statements on a scale from 1 to 7, where a 1 means you *strongly disagree* with the statement and a 7 means you *strongly agree* with it. Place your response in the blanks provided next to each item.

---

* Reprinted with permission of Dr. Susan Sprecher, Illinois State University, Normal, Illinois.

____   1. I need to know someone for a period of time before I fall in love with him or her.

____   2. If I were in love with someone, I would commit myself to him or her even if my parents and friends disapproved of the relationship.

____   3. Once I experience "true love," I could never experience it again, to the same degree, with another person.

____   4. I believe that to be truly in love is to be in love forever.

____   5. If I love someone, I know I can make the relationship work, despite any obstacles.

____   6. When I find my "true love" I will probably know it soon after we meet.

____   7. I'm sure that every new thing I learn about the person I choose for a long-term commitment will please me.

____   8. The relationship I will have with my "true love" will be nearly perfect.

____   9. If I love someone, I will find a way for us to be together regardless of the opposition to the relationship, physical distance between us, or any other barrier.

____ 10. There will be only one real love for me.

____ 11. If a relationship I have was meant to be, any obstacle (e.g., lack of money, physical distance, career conflicts) can be overcome.

____ 12. I am likely to fall in love almost immediately if I meet the right person.

____ 13. I expect that in my relationship, romantic love will really last; it won't fade with time.

____ 14. The person I love will make a perfect romantic partner; for example, he/she will be completely accepting, loving, and understanding.

____ 15. I believe if another person and I love each other, we can overcome any differences and problems that may arise.

Scale of 1 to 7
1 = Strongly disagree; 7 = Strongly agree

SCORING

There are four subscales to the Romantic Beliefs Scale. They are (1) Love Finds a Way (LFW), (2) the One and Only (OO), (3) Idealization (I), and (4) Love at First Sight (LFS). To find your score on each subscale, sum your responses to each item on each subscale. The items that belong to each subscale are as follows:

LFW	OO	I	LFS
2	3	7	1
5	4	8	6
9	10	14	12
11			
13			
15			

HOW DO YOU COMPARE?

LFW	OO	I	LFS	TOTAL	PERCENTILE
39	16	14	15	84	85
34	14	12	12	72	70
30	11	10	10	61	50
26	8	8	8	50	30
21	6	6	5	38	15

High scores indicate stronger beliefs in the concept in question. If, for instance, you received a percentile score of 30 on the OO scale, it means that 30 percent of people have a less strong belief than you do in the One and Only dimension.

For more information, see Susan Sprecher and Sandra Metts, "Development of the Romantic Beliefs Scale and Examination of the Effects of Gender and

Gender-Role Orientation," *Journal of Social and Personal Relationships* 6 (1989): 387–411.

ABOUT THE ROMANTIC BELIEFS SCALE

I admit it. I liked the movie *Sabrina*. For those of you who did not see it, Harrison Ford plays the role of a multibillionaire businessman named Linus Larabbee, who falls in love with the chauffeur's daughter, Sabrina, played by Julia Ormond. He tries to ignore his feelings, because they simply do not make any sense to him. After all, he is considerably older than she, and he is responsible for the family business. He does not have time for love.

Near the end of the movie, Linus tells Sabrina that he was lying when he expressed his love for her earlier. He says that he did it to keep his younger brother from jilting his fiancée—the daughter of another multibillionaire businessman—for Sabrina and ruining a zillion dollar merger. Sabrina, of course, is heartbroken. With tears in her eyes, she says goodbye to Linus and leaves for the airport. After such humiliation, her only recourse is to leave the country. Linus's brother and mother both tell him what a fool he is to let Sabrina leave. He is finally convinced. He gives in to his heart, he catches the Concorde so that he can make it to Paris before Sabrina, and we all have a warm, fuzzy feeling when the two of them are reunited. After all, what could be more important than love?

While most of us applaud Linus's decision, many of us would behave quite differently in real life. We would tell ourselves that it is pure folly to marry someone twenty years younger than we are. And how many of us would be willing to risk a zillion dollar deal for our one, true love. As warm as I felt when Linus finally had Sabrina in his arms again, in real life, I would stick around to close the deal.

Although only the most cynical and hard-hearted people would pooh-pooh romance in the movies, psychological research has demonstrated that the degree to which we hold romantic beliefs varies greatly from person to person. The first tests designed to measure one's adherence to a romantic ideal, as it has been called, are nearly a half-century old. One of the most recent and best of these tests is the Romantic Beliefs Inventory, developed by sociologists Susan Sprecher and Sandra Metts. Their scale yields a total score, as well as individual scores on the dimensions of Love Finds a Way, the One and Only, Idealization, and Love at First Sight.

One of the most interesting questions regarding the romantic ideal, and one that Sprecher and Metts address, is whether men or women are the more romantic sex. The early studies, conducted in the 1950s and 1960s, resulted in a resounding vote for men. Men were more likely to believe notions such as "the one and only" and "love conquers all." Women, it seemed, were much more practical about it all. In one study, a majority of women committed romantic heresy when they indicated that they would consider marrying a man who possessed all the qualities they were looking for even if they were not in love with him.

The conventional wisdom among the experts during the 1970s and 1980s was that this difference between men and women in the degree to which they subscribed to the romantic ideal was destined to disappear. The argument was that 1950s women were forced to be practical in their choice of a partner. Because their standard of living was largely dependent on the man they mar-ried, they simply did not have the luxury of being romantic. The experts told us that as women began to pursue their own careers in the 1970s and achieve finan-cial independence, they could indulge themselves and base their choice of a partner on romance. Well, accord-ing to Sprecher and Metts, it hasn't happened yet. Men received significantly higher scores than women on the overall total and on three of the four specific dimen-sions of the Romantic Beliefs Scale. The only exception was the One and Only scale, on which men and women received similar scores.

It may come as a surprise to learn that there is sci-entific evidence that men are more romantic than women. After all, we all know that women like romance magazines while men would rather browse through *Mechanics Illustrated*. We know romantic come-dies are made with women in mind while the latest Arnold Schwarzenagger movie is aimed directly at men. So, how could it be possible that men are more romantic than women?

The best answer I have heard came from a nontra-ditional student (this is campus jargon that means she was older than twenty-five) in my human sexuality class. She said, "Sure, men are plenty romantic before they know they have you. They love dim light then. They want to spend every night taking you for candlelit dinners followed by moonlit walks on the beach. But after they have you, the only dim light they are inter-ested in is the glow from the television screen."

This woman's observation is consistent with what I've heard from couples in marital counseling. No matter how romantic they were while dating, after the marriage ceremony, most men have trouble seeing the point of romance. Their wives will tell them, "Why don't we plan to do something romantic this weekend?" The men will ask, with genuine puzzlement, "How can you 'plan' to be romantic? Romance has to be spontaneous, it can't be served up on demand, like a fast-food hamburger."

Not only are men and women different in the level to which they accept the romantic idea, they seem to be different in how they view the role of romance. Men tend to view it as a means to an end. They are motivated to be romantic when it means it will help them capture the heart of the woman they love. Women, on the other hand, tend to view romance as the icing on the cake of any relationship. Even if they have been with their partner for several decades and are completely secure in the relationship, they continue to crave those romantic moments for their own sake. Indeed, the most common motive for women who have extramarital affairs is not sexual, but rather the desire for romance and intimacy. Men would be well advised to keep this in mind.

An important question about the Romantic Beliefs Scale is whether it can predict the course of relationships. Sprecher and Metts stated that an important goal of the development of this scale was to inspire research to answer this question. But as of now, we have little scientific evidence about the correlation between adherence to romantic beliefs and relationship satisfaction. Despite the absence of empirical data, most experts agree that too many romantic notions can lead to trouble. This strikes me as being especially true for the Idealization dimension, represented by Item 14, which mentions a partner who is completely accepting, loving, and understanding. Everyone who has been in a long-term relationship recognizes this for the romantic nonsense it is, but I have seen many people in therapy who were ready to leave their partners the first time they discovered that they were not completely accepting, loving, and understanding.

I suspect the "best" scores on this test are near the middle. Extremely low scores suggest to me people who have no romance in their souls, a deficit that I would not find very appealing. Extremely high scores, on the other hand, probably reflect a rather Pollyannish view of relationships—a view that is bound to result in disappointment. Until researchers provide hard evidence about this issue, I would recommend enough romanticism to keep the relationship interesting but enough realism to keep it stable.

CHAPTER TEN

The Love Ways Inventory

The following list of statements describes how people experience love and the ways in which lovers express their feelings for each other. Respond to each item using a 7-point scale, where a 7 *describes very well* and a 1 *does not describe* how you feel. Use the numbers 2 through 6 for statements that fall between these two points in the accuracy with which they describe your situation.

---

* Reprinted with permission of Dr. Michael L. Hecht, Arizona State University, Tempe, Arizona.

___ 1. My partner's love is expressed through physical contact.

___ 2. My partner's love is expressed through the way he/she looks at me.

___ 3. I express my love non-verbally.

___ 4. My partner's love is expressed sexually.

___ 5. I express my love by the way I look at my partner.

___ 6. I express my love sexually.

___ 7. My love's love is expressed through his/her facial expression.

___ 8. I express my love physically through touch.

___ 9. My partner's love is expressed through the intimate topics he/she discusses with me.

___ 10. My partner's love is expressed through the sound of his/her voice.

___ 11. Love is a feeling of togetherness, connectedness, and sharing.

___ 12. Love means being able to communicate freely and easily with my partner.

___ 13. Love is doing things together.

___ 14. Love makes me feel passionate.

___ 15. Love makes me feel secure.

___ 16. Love means that he/she needs me.

___ 17. Love makes me feel confident and self-assured.

___ 18. Love makes me feel healthier and more complete.

___ 19. My partner's love is expressed through his/her need for me.

___ 20. Love makes me feel healthy.

Scale of 1 to 7

1 = Does not describe how you feel; 7 = Describes very well how you feel

___ 21. Love makes me feel anxious.

___ 22. Love makes me feel strong.

___ 23. Love makes me lose my appetite.

___ 24. Love makes me feel nervous.

___ 25. Love gives me energy.

___ 26. Love makes me feel warm.

___ 27. My partner's love is expressed by discussing the future with me.

___ 28. I express my love by planning the future with my partner.

___ 29. My partner's love is expressed through his/her commitment to me.

___ 30. I express my love by making a commitment.

___ 31. My partner's love is expressed by telling me, "I love you."

Scale of 1 to 7
1 = Does not describe how you feel; 7 = Describes very well how you feel

SCORING

The Love Ways Inventory is scored for five subscales. To find your score on each scale, simply add together your responses to the relevant items. The scales, and the items that fall on each scale, are as follows:

Intuitive Love	Items 1–9
Companionate Love	Items 10–14
Secure Love	Items 15–19
Traditional Love	Items 20–26
Committed Love	Items 27–31

HOW DO YOU COMPARE?

INTUITIVE	COMPANIONATE	SECURE	TRADITIONAL	COMMITTED	PERCENTILE
47	27	25	40	28	85
44	25	23	37	25	70
40	22	20	34	22	50
36	19	17	31	19	30
33	17	15	28	16	15

A high score means that you have high levels of the quality in question. If, for example, you received a percentile score of 70 on the Secure scale, it means that 70 percent of people scored lower than you did in that dimension.

For more information, see Michael L. Hecht, Peter J. Marston, and Linda K. Larkey, "Love Ways and Relationship Quality in Heterosexual Relationships," *Journal of Social and Personal Relationships* 11 (1994): 25–43.

ABOUT THE LOVE WAYS INVENTORY

"How do I love thee? Let me count the ways," Elizabeth Barrett Browning said. Well, psychologists have been counting up the ways themselves, and as you can tell from the number of tests in this section, they have come up with quite a list.

It should come as no surprise that love has been the focus of so much research. Love, as well as the relationships that result from this powerful emotion, plays a critical role in the satisfaction we derive from life. If we manage this emotion wisely and respond to its best elements, we can have relationships that enrich our existence and make life seem worthwhile. If we make poor decisions and let the worst elements of love rule our lives, we may experience much frustration, disappointment, and even despair. If we are to have gratifying relationships, it is critical that we understand how the emotion of love affects us, and how we can best manage its powerful forces. Michael Hecht, Peter Marston, and Linda Larkey, with their Love Ways Inventory, have provided an instrument that can help us understand this powerful emotion.

Hecht and his colleagues concluded that there were five basic "love ways"—the five dimensions for which you could score the results of your test. The first dimension, Intuitive Love, is associated with a variety of bodily sensations, such as feelings of warmth and sexual responsiveness. Committed Love is experienced by a couple when they spend time together and communicate their desire to have a future together. The third dimension, Secure Love, is characterized by feelings of security and is expressed by sharing one's innermost feelings and by doing favors for one's partner.

Companionate Love describes the feeling of connectedness that couples share and the desire to share everything that life has to offer. And finally, Traditional, or
Romantic, Love includes the feelings most people have
when they first fall "in love"—that is, feelings of being
attractive, desirable, and full of energy, along with a
feeling of nervousness so often described by lovers as
butterflies in the stomach.

Hecht and his colleagues conceptualized love
slightly differently from most other researchers. Rather
than viewing these five dimensions as relatively dis-
crete and independent, they emphasized that they
could combine in an almost countless number of per-
mutations. Drawing from the writings of existentialists
such as Sartre, they maintained that these dimensions
coalesce to form a holistic experience that may be different from lover to lover. And their primary interest
was in learning if the specific Love Ways of partners
affected the quality of their relationship.

The results of their research were extremely complex, and it will take a number of additional studies to
properly sort things out. But there were several findings that are worth thinking about when you try to
understand your relationship. First, and perhaps most
surprising, was the finding that for four of the dimensions, there was almost no correspondence in partners'
Love Ways. Once a relationship has been established,
there is a tendency for us to assume that our partner
feels about us the same way we feel about him or her
and an even stronger tendency to believe that "true
love" means that our partner *should* feel about us the
way we feel about him or her. This does not necessarily happen. Women, for instance, who defined their

relationship in terms of Companionate Love, did not necessarily have partners who conceptualized their love in the same way.

However, in the Committed Love dimension, partners tended to respond similarly. Furthermore, for both men and women, scores on this dimension had the strongest association with overall satisfaction with the relationship. It is impossible to know at this point, however, whether couples who express their feelings for each other primarily in terms of Committed Love consequently have a better relationship or whether couples who have a satisfying relationship develop a stronger sense of commitment to each other. In other words, we don't know what comes first—the chicken or the egg.

So how important is it for couples to have the same Love Ways? The answer is that it depends. There was no evidence that it was important with respect to Intuitive, Traditional (Romantic), or Committed Love, but similarity of Love Ways did play a role in relationship satisfaction with regard to Companionate and Secure Love.

To illustrate, consider the case of Tom and Anne. Tom's feelings for Anne are reflected in his very high scores on both the Companionate and Secure Love scales. He believes that people who love each other should spend most of their free time together and that they should be willing to grant most any favor their partner asks of them. Anne, on the other hand, feels completely committed to her husband, but his desire for the two of them to share all aspects of their lives makes her feel claustrophobic at times. She would love to spend a long weekend in New York with a couple of her friends, and she would love it if Tom would take a golf or fishing trip with his friends every now and then. But Tom refuses to go anywhere overnight without Anne, and the one time Anne planned a trip of her own, Tom was so upset that she decided it was not worth the hurt feelings.

Tom and Anne will stay married, I'm sure of that. But Anne will always view her husband as somewhat neurotic and needy. At times she will even feel mildly disgusted by his seeming inability to function independently for even a few days. Tom will continue to worry and sometimes feel quite depressed by the belief that Anne does not love him as much as he loves her. If she really did, he says, she would not want to be apart from him, even for a few days.

Because the "Ways" associated with Companionate Love and Secure Love reflect the degree of togetherness and connectedness a couple seeks from the relationship, differences on these dimensions can cause problems. Tom and Anne's differences on these dimensions are not so pronounced that they have destroyed their relationship, but nonetheless, they have caused them both to experience less satisfaction than they otherwise might. Through counseling, they have managed to achieve some appreciation for the simple but painful fact that they view love differently. So, Tom tells himself that just because Anne would like to go off with friends for a few days does not mean that she does not love him. And Anne no longer tells Tom that his "neediness" and dependency must reflect a "screwed-up" childhood. But they both continue to experience moments when they relapse.

This is clearly a case where an ounce of prevention is worth a pound of cure. The best way to avoid a situation like Tom and Anne's is to find someone with Love Ways similar to your own. I think most people have a sense of these differences before they make a commitment, but they choose to ignore them believing that their partner will change with time. While they were dating, Tom was often hurt when Anne told him she could not see him because she had made plans with friends. But he was certain that once they were married, her desire to spend time with anyone else would fade away. And Anne was annoyed by Tom's hurt feelings when she informed him of plans that did not include him, but she was confident that he would not be so demanding after they were married and they spent most of their free time with each other. As Tom and Anne learned, perhaps people can change, but they rarely change as much as we would like them to.

Psychological tests are far from perfect, and I would never advise a couple to forget their relationship simply because they had quite different scores on Companionate and Secure Love Ways. I would tell them that love does not mean that a couple has to feel exactly the same way about each other. However, I would advise them to be sensitive to their differences and to remind themselves frequently about them. Tom and Anne have had to struggle to understand each other at times, but overall, both of them find their relationship deeply satisfying.

CHAPTER ELEVEN

The Love Attitudes Scale

The following list of statements reflects different attitudes about love. For each statement, fill in the response in the blank next to the item that indicates how much you agree or disagree with that statement. The items refer to a specific love relationship. Whenever possible, answer the questions with your current partner in mind. If you are not currently dating anyone, answer the questions with your most recent partner in mind. If you have never been in love, answer in terms of what you think your responses would most likely be.

    5 = Strongly agree with the statement
    4 = Moderately agree with the statement
    3 = Neutral (neither agree nor disagree)
    2 = Moderately disagree with the statement
    1 = Strongly disagree with the statement

---

* Reprinted with permission of Clyde Hendrick, Texas Tech University, Lubbock, Texas.

___ 1. My partner and I were attracted to each other immediately after we first met.

___ 2. My partner and I have the right physical "chemistry" between us.

___ 3. Our lovemaking is very intense and satisfying.

___ 4. I feel that my partner and I were meant for each other.

___ 5. My partner and I became emotionally involved rather quickly.

___ 6. My partner and I really understand each other.

___ 7. My partner fits my ideal standards of physical beauty/handsomeness.

___ 8. I try to keep my partner a little uncertain about my commitment to him/her.

___ 9. I believe that what my partner doesn't know about me won't hurt him/her.

___ 10. I have sometimes had to keep my partner from finding out about other partners.

___ 11. I could get over my affair with my partner pretty easily and quickly.

___ 12. My partner would get upset if he/she knew of some of the things I've done with other people.

___ 13. When my partner gets too dependent on me, I want to back off a little.

___ 14. I enjoy playing the "game of love" with my partner and a number of other partners.

___ 15. It is hard for me to say exactly when our friendship turned into love.

5 = Strongly agree; 4 = Moderately agree; 3 = Neutral;
2 = Moderately disagree; 1 = Strongly disagree

___ 16. To be genuine, our love first requires "caring" for a while.

___ 17. I expect to always be friends with my partner.

___ 18. Our love is the best kind because it grew out of a long friendship.

___ 19. Our friendship merged gradually into love over time.

___ 20. Our love is really a deep friendship, not a mysterious, mystical emotion.

___ 21. Our love relationship is the most satisfying because it developed from a good friendship.

___ 22. I considered what my partner was going to become in life before I committed myself to him/her.

___ 23. I tried to plan my life carefully before choosing my partner.

___ 24. In choosing my partner, I believed it was best to love someone with a similar background.

___ 25. A main consideration in choosing my partner was how he/she would reflect on my family.

___ 26. An important factor in choosing my partner was whether or not he/she would be a good parent.

___ 27. One consideration in choosing my partner was how he/she would reflect on my career.

___ 28. Before getting very involved with my partner, I tried to figure out how compatible his/her hereditary background would be with mine in case we ever had children.

___ 29. When things aren't right with my partner and me, my stomach gets upset.

5 = Strongly agree; 4 = Moderately agree; 3 = Neutral;
2 = Moderately disagree; 1 = Strongly disagree

___ 30. If my partner and I break up, I would get so depressed that I would even think of suicide.

___ 31. Sometimes I get so excited about being in love with my partner that I can't sleep.

___ 32. When my partner doesn't pay attention to me, I get sick all over.

___ 33. Since I've been in love with my partner, I've had trouble concentrating on anything else.

___ 34. I cannot relax if I suspect that my partner is with someone else.

___ 35. If my partner ignores me for a while, I sometimes do stupid things to try to get his/her attention back.

___ 36. I try to always help my partner through difficult times.

___ 37. I would rather suffer myself than let my partner suffer.

___ 38. I cannot be happy unless I place my partner's happiness before my own.

___ 39. I am usually willing to sacrifice my own wishes to let my partner achieve his/hers.

___ 40. Whatever I own is my partner's to use as he/she chooses.

___ 41. When my partner gets angry with me, I still love him/her fully and unconditionally.

___ 42. I would endure all things for the sake of my partner.

5 = Strongly agree; 4 = Moderately agree; 3 = Neutral;
2 = Moderately disagree; 1 = Strongly disagree

SCORING

There are six subscales to the Love Attitudes Scale. They are (1) Eros (E), (2) Ludus (L), (3) Pragma (P), (4) Storge (S), (5) Mania (M), and (6) Agape (A). To find your score on each subscale, sum your responses to each item on each subscale. The items belonging to each subscale are as follows:

Eros	Items 1–7
Ludus	Items 8–14
Pragma	Items 15–21
Storge	Items 22–28
Mania	Items 29–35
Agape	Items 36–42

HOW DO YOU COMPARE?

E	L	P	S	M	A	PERCENTILE
21	33	24	30	29	21	85
18	29	20	26	25	18	70
15	25	17	22	21	15	50
12	21	14	18	17	12	30
9	17	10	14	13	9	15

High scores indicate higher levels of the characteristic in question. If, for example, you received a percentile score of 85 on S, it means that 85 percent of people scored lower than you did in levels of Storge.

For more information, see Clyde Hendrick and Susan Hendrick, "A Theory and Method of Love," *Journal of Personality and Social Psychology* 50 (1986): 392–402.

About the Love Attitudes Scale

Clyde and Susan Hendrick, a husband and wife team of psychologists, have taken perhaps the most comprehensive look at love. They carefully reviewed a number of theories of love and attempted to develop a scale that would represent an integration of these theories. Their work was extremely fruitful and has resulted in the Love Attitudes Scale. The scale measured the six dimensions for which you scored the results of your test. Let us begin by taking a look at what these dimensions mean.

Eros involves the physical side of love. It is intensely emotional and results in a strong attraction to the lover early in the relationship. People experiencing eros value love greatly and usually have a strong commitment to their lovers.

Ludus lovers are those who crave the "game" of love, preferably with several partners. This type of person views deception as an acceptable and sometimes even necessary part of the dance of love. These people tend to be manipulative and are often wary of deep emotional intensity on the part of their lovers. The Hendricks point out that while some people's style is characterized primarily by Ludus, there are ludic aspects to most love relationships.

Storge represents a merger of love and friendship. Storge does not have the fire of eros; it is a dependable, down-to-earth kind of love. It evolves over the course of a relationship and may be the bond that keeps couples together over the long term after eros has begun to lose its power.

Pragma describes an objective search for the qualities we want in our lovers. The Hendricks called Pragma lovers "computer mating" people because they seemed to approach relationships with a predefined checklist of the characteristics they wanted in a partner. Needless to say, this type of love tends to be low in emotional intensity.

Mania is a frantic, insecure love style. People who experience mania tend to have poor self-esteem and are often tormented with uncertainty about their lover's commitment to them. Adolescents, who are just beginning to take part in the dance of love, may be especially likely to experience Mania, but the Hendricks note that it is far from uncommon in older lovers.

Agape is a selfless, altruistic kind of love. Agape lovers are willing to make all manner of sacrifices for their partner, never expecting anything in return. Interestingly, people who reported "being in love now" when they took the test scored significantly higher on Agape than those men and women who were not in love. Perhaps one has to be consumed with the emotions of love before one can even imagine making such sacrifices.

One important issue, both from a theoretical and practical view, is whether these love types reflect stable personality characteristics or whether they can vary from relationship to relationship for the same person. In other words, if Ludus best describes your current relationship, are you destined to a lifetime of ludic relationships, or is there something unique about your current relationship that has made it ludic? The Hendricks suggest this is a critical question for future researchers to explore, but they speculate that "some of both" is probably the best answer.

We do know that people tend to be consistent in their levels of emotional intensity, so it is likely that those who have highly charged affairs are prone to the more emotionally intense kinds of love—namely, Eros and Mania. People who do not have intense emotional reactions may be more prone to experience Ludus, Storge, or Pragma. It does seem unlikely that a person who tends to have intense reactions to a variety of situations could ever become a "computer mating" or Pragma lover.

On the other hand, there is good reason to believe that the kind of love one experiences can vary from relationship to relationship. Consider for a moment the middle-aged man who announces to his wife of thirty years, "I love you, but I am in love with someone else." The Hendricks acknowledge that it may be possible to have simultaneous relationships that are characterized by different kinds of love. So our middle-aged Lothario may be telling his wife the truth. His relationship with her may be characterized by Storge and Pragma, but his relationship with his mistress may be pure Eros. Because Eros is such an intense experience and one that includes a strong sense of commitment, he may consider "giving up everything" for his new lover. In the end, his decision may be determined by his typical style. If he is a highly emotional person, he may give in to the Eros. If he is a calm, rational type, the Storge and Pragma may prevail.

Comparing your partner's love style with your own is important because we know that an important predictor of satisfying, long-term relationships is the similarity of love styles. If you characterize your relationship as being dominated by Eros, for example, while your partner views it as Pragma, both of you are likely to experience some frustration. You will want more romance, physical affection, and emotional intimacy than your partner is either willing or able to give you. In turn, your partner may feel suffocated by your constant demands for his or her attention.

These differences are not likely to be a problem unless they are pronounced. So, for example, there is no need to worry if your Eros score was the highest and your partner's Pragma score was the highest, as long as your partner had a strong showing on the Eros scale. You might want to think hard about a future with your partner, however, if the two of you had very different love profiles. The odds would be against you if you scored above the 85th percentile on Eros and your partner scored below the 15th percentile.

A high score on the Ludus scale is a clear danger signal. If your partner scored higher than the 85th percentile on this dimension (especially if he or she is dense enough to let you see the score), you are probably in for some painful times. These people report being in love significantly more often than their low Ludus counterparts, and they tend to avoid emotional commitment. If they do not currently have another lover, the odds are good they will before long.

If you scored higher than the 85th percentile on Ludus, you may want to think long and hard about whether this style will serve you well in the long run.

The conventional wisdom among mental health professionals is that such people are deficient in their ability to form close, meaningful relationships, and consequently are destined to a life of emptiness and loneliness. I'm not sure I would go that far. I have known many people who, before settling down, had numerous ludic relationships with no apparent psychological scars. I have known a few people who made it into their sixties and seventies without ever having a relationship (including a few marriages) that wasn't ludic, and they have no regrets. I believe there are some people who simply do not need the same stability that most of us crave. And these people seem perfectly satisfied with their ludic relationships.

On the other hand, I have known more people (especially in the context of psychotherapy) whose relationships were characterized by Ludus and who were miserable as a result. They wanted to change, but they seemed addicted to the excitement of their love games. Once their partners began to express a wish for something more solid and stable, they bolted and began their search for a new "fix."

There are no easy answers for such people because they are at odds with themselves. They want to have it both ways, but it is nearly impossible to find a partner who is willing to go along with this plan. If you find yourself in one ludic relationship after another but wonder why you cannot find emotional intimacy and stability, consider finding a good therapist to help you work out this conflict.

CHAPTER TWELVE

The Attitudes Toward Love Scale

Please read each statement carefully, and enter the number that you believe most adequately represents your opinion.

1 = Strongly agree (definitely yes)
2 = Mildly agree (I believe so)
3 = Undecided (not sure)
4 = Mildly disagree (probably not)
5 = Strongly disagree (definitely not)

* Reprinted with permission of Dr. David Knox Jr., East Carolina University, Greenville, North Carolina.

___ 1. When you are really in love, you just aren't interested in anyone else.

___ 2. Love doesn't make sense. It just is.

___ 3. When you fall head over heels in love, it's sure to be the real thing.

___ 4. Love isn't anything you can really study; it is too highly emotional to be subject to scientific observation.

___ 5. To be in love with someone without marriage is a tragedy.

___ 6. When love hits, you know it.

___ 7. Common interests are really unimportant; as long as each of you is truly in love, you will adjust.

___ 8. It doesn't matter if you marry after you have known your partner for only a short time as long as you know you are in love.

___ 9. As long as two people love each other, the religious differences they have really do not matter.

___ 10. You can love someone even though you do not like any of that person's friends.

___ 11. When you are in love, you are usually in a daze.

___ 12. Love at first sight is often the deepest and most enduring type of love.

___ 13. Usually there are only one or two people in the world whom you could really love and with whom you could really be happy.

___ 14. Regardless of other factors, if you truly love another person, that is enough to marry that person.

___ 15. To be happy, it is necessary to be in love with the one you marry.

1 = Strongly agree; 2 = Mildly agree; 3 = Undecided;
4 = Mildly disagree; 5 = Strongly disagree

____ 16. When you are separated from the love partner, the rest of the world seems dull and unsatisfying.

____ 17. Parents should not advise their children whom to date; they have forgotten what it is like to be in love.

____ 18. Love is regarded as a primary motive for marriage, which is good.

____ 19. When you love a person, you think of marrying that person.

____ 20. Somewhere there is an ideal mate for most people. The problem is finding that one.

____ 21. Jealousy usually varies directly with love; that is, the more in love you are, the greater the tendency for you to become jealous.

____ 22. Love is best described as an exciting thing rather than a calm thing.

____ 23. There are probably only a few people that any one person can fall in love with.

____ 24. When you are in love, your judgment is usually not too clear.

____ 25. Love often comes but once in a lifetime.

____ 26. You can't make yourself love someone; it just comes or it doesn't.

____ 27. As compared with love, differences in social class and religion are of small importance in selecting a marriage partner.

____ 28. Daydreaming usually comes along with being in love.

____ 29. When you are in love, you don't have to ask yourself a bunch of questions about love; you will just know that you are in love.

1 = Strongly agree; 2 = Mildly agree; 3 = Undecided;
4 = Mildly disagree; 5 = Strongly disagree

SCORING

To calculate your total score, simply add your responses to the items.

HOW DO YOU COMPARE?

MEN	WOMEN	PERCENTILE
108	113	85
101	106	70
94	99	50
87	92	30
80	85	15

Scores above the 50th percentile indicate conjugal love. Scores below the 50th percentile indicate romantic love.

For more information, see David H. Knox Jr. and Michael J. Sporakowski, "Attitudes of College Students Toward Love," *Journal of Marriage and the Family* 30 (1968): 683–642.

ABOUT THE ATTITUDES TOWARD LOVE SCALE

As we have seen from the first five tests in this section, there are clear differences among people in how they view love. Nonetheless, it is probably fair to say that most of us do tend to subscribe, at least to some extent, to the romantic ideal. At the very least, we will nod our heads approvingly when we hear a friend say something like, "If they really love each other, they can work it out." And we shake our heads disapprovingly when we hear about the beautiful young woman who married the elderly billionaire. We can't believe she married for love, and any other motive, especially one so crass as the acquisition of wealth, just isn't right.

Despite our romantic ideals, most of us end up making reasonably realistic choices. The scientific evidence is overwhelming that we tend to marry someone who comes from a background similar to our own and who shares our views on religion, work, children, politics—the list could go on and on. We may have a soft spot for movies and novels about the rich girl who marries the boy from the wrong side of the tracks, but we are not likely to do something like that ourselves. Perhaps social scientist Morton Hunt captured this paradox best: "Americans are firmly of two minds about it all, simultaneously hardhearted and idealistic, uncouth and tender, libidinous and puritanical. They believe implicitly in every tenet of romantic love and yet they know perfectly well that things don't really work that way."

Marriage counselors David Knox and Michael Sporakowski were interested in capturing this paradox with their Attitudes Toward Love Scale, and they were quite successful at it. Their test can be described as a bipolar scale in that a low score reflects a strong belief in what they call Romantic Love and a high score reflects their concept of Conjugal Love. We've discussed romantic love in the preceding chapters. It is the highly charged, emotional kind of love that demands that lovers be totally involved, even obsessed with each other. Conjugal love describes the bond between two settled people. It is calm, solid, and more firmly grounded in reality. Conjugal love goes beyond chemistry—it describes two people who mesh emotionally, intellectually, and spiritually.

An especially interesting finding from Knox and Sporakowski's research was that older men and women became more realistic—that is, they had higher levels of Conjugal Love—than their younger counterparts. As the researchers suggested, this could reflect a tendency to "give up" one's romantic notions as one approaches the age at which settling down becomes an attractive option. It is okay to experience all the emotional thrills love has to offer when young, but as people begin to think about selecting a partner for life, they realize they have to be realistic in their judgments. This possibility was supported by the finding that engaged men had more realistic views about love than did their nonengaged peers. Again, they may feel free to indulge in the excitement of romantic love when they are footloose and fancy free—when the consequences of making a poor choice are not especially severe. But when they become serious about selecting a spouse, they take off their rose-colored glasses to reduce the possibility that they will make a serious mistake. As Knox and Sporakowski reported and as other researchers have found, women had more realistic views of love than did men. While women clearly experience all the thrills associated with romantic love, it seems as if they always keep one eye at least half open.

It may be instructive for you to compare your score on specific items on this test with that of your partner. Let me mention two that strike me as especially important. The first is Item 21. It suggests that jealousy and love are directly related. We have all known people who argue that their own intense jealousy is proof of how much they love their partners, and we have even known men and women (more often women) who tolerate their partners' jealousy because they accept the notion that jealousy and love are inextricably intertwined.

Perhaps it is true that most of us will feel at least a few pangs of jealousy early in a relationship when we see our partner having an animated conversation with someone else, especially if that someone else is more attractive than we are. And it is undoubtedly the case that most of us would feel jealous if our partner of many years began to have long, hushed phone conversations with an unknown person. But the problem with jealousy is that people who see it as an inevitable component of love usually are not very rational about their reactions.

Stewart learned this the hard way when he retired from a career in the Navy and decided to sell real estate part time. As a result of the frequent moves required by his military career, he had purchased and sold a number of houses, and he always enjoyed the process. He believed that as a real-estate agent, he could have enough flexibility in his schedule to fully enjoy his semiretired status.

To his wife's distress, Stewart's new career meant that he was spending a lot of time with other women. More than three fourths of the agents in his office were women, and his job demanded that Stewart talk with them on the phone and meet with them regularly. His wife, Fran, could not stand it. She was convinced that most of her husband's colleagues were intent on stealing him away from her, especially those agents who were single mothers. Fran began to "forget" to give her husband phone messages and demanded that Stewart forgo the office Christmas party; in her mind, the combination of alcohol, single mothers, and her husband could only lead to disaster.

Stewart, of course, was not flattered by his wife's jealousy. He did not interpret it as a sign of how much she loved him, but rather, he felt suffocated by her reactions. The more she protested his meetings with his female colleagues, the more he withdrew from her. This set off a vicious cycle because his withdrawal served to confirm Fran's worst fears. She became even more jealous, and thus Stewart became more intent on avoiding his wife's accusations by putting off the time when he had to return home.

I am not sure that anything can destroy a relationship faster than jealousy. If either you or your partner responded with a "1" for this item, I strongly advise you to work out this issue before going further with your relationship.

Item 10 is also worth mentioning. It states that you can love someone even though you do not like any of that person's friends. When our rose-colored glasses are firmly in place, it may help us to get a clear idea of what our partner is like by taking a close look at his or her friends. The intensity of our feelings may make it impossible to be objective about our true love, but we have no such difficulty when evaluating other people. A cliché worth keeping in mind is that birds of a feather flock together. Behavioral scientists have found that this applies to same-sex friends as well as to romantic partners. So, if you don't like any of your partner's friends, you may discover that once the intensity of the romantic love dissipates, you don't much like your partner. It is a good bet that your partner has many of the same qualities as his or her friends, otherwise they would not be flocking together. I have heard people suggest that if you want to know what your partner will be like in twenty or thirty years, look at his or her same-sex parent. There may be some truth to this idea, but I believe that friends can provide you with an even better opportunity to make an objective assessment of what your partner is like. After all, we do not choose our parents, but we have friends because we like them. And the reality is that we tend to like people who are similar to ourselves.

Making Love

After taking the tests in Part III, you will understand your feelings about your sexuality, your sexual relationship, and your ability to talk about sex with your partner. The following tests are included in Part III:

CHAPTER THIRTEEN

The Sexuality Scale

The following statements describe certain attitudes toward human sexuality that different people may have. As such, there are no right or wrong answers, only personal responses. For each statement, indicate how much you agree or disagree by using the following scale:

5 = Agree
4 = Slightly agree
3 = Neither agree nor disagree
2 = Slightly disagree
1 = Disagree

* Reprinted with permission of Dr. William E. Snell Jr., Southeast Missouri State University, Cape Girardeau, Missouri.

___ 1. I am a good sexual partner.

___ 2. I am depressed about the sexual aspects of my life.

___ 3. I think about sex all the time.

___ 4. I would rate my sexual skill quite highly.

___ 5. I feel good about my sexuality.

___ 6. I think about sex more than anything else.

___ 7. I am better at sex than most other people.

___ 8. I am disappointed about the quality of my sex life.

___ 9. I don't daydream about sexual situations.

___ 10. I sometimes have doubts about my sexual competence.

___ 11. Thinking about sex makes me happy.

___ 12. I tend to be preoccupied with sex.

___ 13. I am not very confident in sexual encounters.

___ 14. I derive pleasure and enjoyment from sex.

___ 15. I'm constantly thinking about having sex.

___ 16. I think of myself as a very good sexual partner.

___ 17. I feel down about my sex life.

___ 18. I think about sex a great deal of the time.

___ 19. I would rate myself low as a sexual partner.

___ 20. I feel unhappy about my sexual relationships.

___ 21. I seldom think about sex.

___ 22. I am confident about myself as a sexual partner.

___ 23. I feel pleased with my sex life.

5 = Agree; 4 = Slightly agree; 3 = Neither agree nor disagree;
2 = Slightly disagree; 1 = Disagree

___ 24. I hardly ever fantasize about having sex.

___ 25. I am not very confident about my sexual skill.

___ 26. I feel sad when I think about my sexual experiences.

___ 27. I probably think about sex less often than most people.

___ 28. I sometimes doubt my sexual competence.

___ 29. I am not discouraged about sex.

___ 30. I don't think about sex very often.

5 = Agree; 4 = Slightly agree; 3 = Neither agree nor disagree;
2 = Slightly disagree; 1 = Disagree

SCORING

There are three subscales to the Sexuality Scale. They
are (1) Sexual Esteem (SE), (2) Sexual Depression (SD),
and (3) Sexual Preoccupation (SP). To find your score
for each subscale, simply add the values of your
responses after reversing your scores for the appropriate items. The items that belong to each subscale are as
follows:

SE	SD	SP
1	2	3
4	5*	6
7	8	9*
10*	17	12
13*	20	15
16	23*	18
19*	26	21*
22	29*	24*
25*		27*
28*		30*

* The items marked with an asterisk should be reverse scored
  (i.e., 1 = 5, 2 = 4, 3 = 3, 4 = 2, and 5 = 1).

HOW DO YOU COMPARE?

SE		SD		SP		
M	F	M	F	M	F	PERCENTILE
45	44	27	25	39	34	85
40	40	22	22	36	30	70
36	36	18	18	32	26	50
32	32	14	14	28	22	30
27	28	9	11	25	18	15

High scores indicate higher levels of the quality in
question. If, for instance, you received a percentile

score of 70 on SD, it means that 70 percent of people have lower levels of sexual depression than do you.

For more information, see William E. Snell Jr. and Dennis R. Papini, "The Sexuality Scale: An Instrument to Measure Sexual-Esteem, Sexual-Depression, and Sexual-Preoccupation," *The Journal of Sex Research* 26 (1989): 256–263.

ABOUT THE SEXUALITY SCALE

If you are like most people, when you think about your sexuality and your sexual experiences, you probably have only a few general reactions. You may have good feelings about your sexuality, or you may wish you felt more comfortable about this critical aspect of human functioning. And you may be pleased with your sexual experiences, or you may wish you could change the quality or quantity of your sexual experiences. In other words, sex isn't all that complicated. Or is it?

Perhaps only psychologists could begin with a relatively straightforward aspect of human behavior and turn it into something extremely complex, but literally hundreds of tests have been developed to measure several dozen aspects of sexual functioning. Much of this work has been done by pure researchers in their attempt to expand knowledge in this area, but much of it has been performed by clinicians who are concerned with helping people improve the quality of their sex lives. One of the most productive of these psychologists, both in terms of quantity and quality of work, is William Snell from Southeastern Missouri State University. Over the past decade, he has headed an ambitious research program that has greatly benefited both researchers and clinicians, and it is his work that we will draw upon in Part III. Let us begin with one of his first instruments, the Sexuality Scale.

As you saw when you scored your responses to this test, the Sexuality Scale is comprised of three subscales that measure Sexual Esteem, Sexual Depression, and Sexual Preoccupation. Sexual Esteem refers to positive feelings about one's ability to relate sexually to another person. People high in Sexual Esteem generally have a keen interest in sex and are sufficiently assertive to establish relationships to satisfy this interest. As you can see from the norms, men have significantly higher scores on this dimension than do women, a difference that may have resulted from men's greater level of sexual experiences. Snell reported that Sexual Esteem was a direct function of experience: People who had more sexual experiences tended to feel better about their sexuality. An alternative explanation for men's higher average score might be that it results from their greater need to view themselves as skilled lovers. Women seem to be more willing to express doubts about their adequacy in this area.

People with high Sexual Esteem have what Snell calls a communal approach to sex. These people approach sexual encounters with a sense of honesty and openness and view them as an activity in which both partners should cooperate to ensure that the experience is mutually pleasurable. People low in Sexual Esteem are more likely to have either an exchange view of sex (i.e., "You do this for me, and I'll do that for you") or believe that it is necessary to manipulate and even deceive a partner to get what one wants.

Sexual Depression, the second scale on this test, is essentially the flip side of Sexual Esteem. It is defined as feelings of sadness and discouragement about one's difficulties in relating sexually to another person. People with high scores on this scale tend to be high in anxiety and guilt about sex and are less likely than their nondepressed peers to be in a relationship. For those sexually depressed people who are in a relationship, there is a rather low level of sexual involvement. They tend to feel insecure about their partners, they do not feel strongly committed to their relationships, and they do not expect their relationships to last long.

Among women who served as subjects for Snell's research, those with high scores on the Sexual Depression scale were different from high scoring men in one very important way. The first sexual experience of these women was likely to have been with a relative. Needless to say, these relationships were described as abusive and were viewed as having a negative influence on their subsequent sexual relationships.

Perhaps to no one's surprise, men received an average score that was more than twice as great as the average score for women on the third scale, Sexual Preoccupation. It would seem that people who scored high on this scale may have been preoccupied with sex because they were sexually deprived. Snell and Papini found that they were less likely than their nonpreoccupied peers to be in a relationship, and they were more sensitive to their sexual feelings. Also, they had high levels of motivation to experience sex, and they tended to have permissive sexual attitudes.

Interestingly, although women who scored high on the Sexual Preoccupation scale had a greater variety of sexual experiences than did low scoring women, the same was not true for men. Perhaps this can be explained by the observation that women are the "gate-keepers" of sexual relationships. This idea, suggested by a number of behavioral scientists, reflects the fact that men do most of the asking while women have the option of saying yes or no. So men who are high in Sexual Preoccupation may ask a lot, but they are probably regularly told no. A sexually preoccupied woman, on the other hand, will probably have less difficulty in finding men who are willing to say yes.

If you had a score lower than the 15th percentile on Sexual Esteem and higher than the 85th percentile of Sexual Depression, be assured that it is not necessary for you to have such negative feelings about your sexuality and your sexual relationships. The first step in changing this aspect of your life is to understand why you have these negative feelings. If you are not currently in a relationship and if you have had difficulty in forming or sustaining relationships, you may want to go back to Part I and review the material there. Perhaps your shyness or your belief that you can do nothing to improve your relationships with others is standing in your way. Once you improve your ability to connect with others, you will probably find that connecting sexually comes rather easily.

If you are in an important relationship now and have low Sexual Esteem and high Sexual Depression, the best place to start is by talking with your partner about your concerns. The last test in Part III, the Sexual Self-Disclosure Scale, is one you will want to pay particular attention to.

If you are a woman and you were the victim of sexual abuse, then a patient, supportive, and understanding partner can work wonders, but it may still not be enough. I believe that in many cases, it is worthwhile to try self-help approaches before consulting a professional therapist, but this is an important exception. If you have already suffered for years from negative feelings about your sexuality, the time to seek professional help is now. You can put your memories behind you and get on with the rest of your life. I urge you to begin as soon as possible.

Unusually high or low levels of Sexual Preoccupation may reflect nothing more than your biological makeup. Most human characteristics fit a bell-shaped curve, and just as some people are taller than average and others are shorter than average, people vary naturally in their level of Sexual Preoccupation or interest.

There are, however, occasions when an unusual degree of Sexual Preoccupation reflects conflicts that can be resolved. If you scored below the 15th percentile on Sexual Preoccupation and you discover, after taking the remaining tests in Part III, that you have unusually high levels of sexual guilt or anxiety, your lack of interest in sex might be your way of keeping your negative feelings to manageable levels. If you scored at the 85th percentile or higher, your strong interest in sex is only a problem if you find yourself engaging in self-destructive sexual behaviors. This problem, sometimes referred to as sexual addiction, is another condition that probably requires that you seek professional help.

CHAPTER FOURTEEN

The Sexual Awareness Questionnaire

The statements that follow refer to the sexual aspects of people's lives. Please read each statement carefully and decide to what extent it is characteristic of you. Give each item a rating of how much it applies to you by using the following scale. (Remember to respond to all items, even if you are not completely sure.)

1 = Not at all characteristic of me
2 = Slightly characteristic of me
3 = Somewhat characteristic of me
4 = Moderately characteristic of me
5 = Very characteristic of me

---

* Reprinted with permission of Dr. William E. Snell Jr., Southeast Missouri State University, Cape Girardeau, Missouri.

___ 1. I am very aware of my sexual feelings.

___ 2. I wonder whether others think I'm sexy.

___ 3. I'm assertive about the sexual aspects of my life.

___ 4. I'm very aware of my sexual motivations.

___ 5. I'm concerned about the sexual appearance of my body.

___ 6. I'm not very direct about voicing my sexual desires.

___ 7. I'm always trying to understand my sexual feelings.

___ 8. I know immediately when others consider me sexy.

___ 9. I am somewhat passive about expressing my sexual desires.

___ 10. I'm very alert to changes in my sexual desires.

___ 11. I am quick to sense whether others think I'm sexy.

___ 12. I do not hesitate to ask for what I want in a sexual relationship.

___ 13. I am very aware of my sexual tendencies.

___ 14. I usually worry about making a good sexual impression on others.

___ 15. I'm the type of person who insists on having my sexual needs met.

___ 16. I think about my sexual motivations more than most people do.

___ 17. I'm concerned about what other people think of my sex appeal.

___ 18. When it comes to sex, I usually ask for what I want.

___ 19. I reflect about my sexual desires a lot.

___ 20. I never seem to know when I'm turning others on.

---

1 = Not at all characteristic of me; 2 = Slightly characteristic of me;
3 = Somewhat characteristic of me;
4 = Moderately characteristic of me; 5 = Very characteristic of me

____ 21. If I were to become sexually interested in someone, I'd let that person know.

____ 22. I'm very aware of the way my mind works when I'm sexually aroused.

____ 23. I rarely think about my sex appeal.

____ 24. If I were to have sex with someone, I'd tell my partner what I like.

____ 25. I know what turns me on sexually.

____ 26. I don't care what others think of my sexuality.

____ 27. I don't let others tell me how to run my sex life.

____ 28. I rarely think about the sexual aspects of my life.

____ 29. I know when others think I'm sexy.

____ 30. If I were to have sex with someone, I'd let my partner take the initiative.

____ 31. I don't think about my sexuality very much.

____ 32. Other people's opinions of my sexuality don't matter very much to me.

____ 33. I would ask about sexually transmitted diseases before having sex with someone.

____ 34. I don't consider myself a very sexual person.

____ 35. When I'm with others, I want to look sexy.

____ 36. If I wanted to practice safe sex with someone, I would insist on doing so.

1 = Not at all characteristic of me; 2 = Slightly characteristic of me;
3 = Somewhat characteristic of me;
4 = Moderately characteristic of me; 5 = Very characteristic of me

Scoring

There are four subscales to the Sexual Awareness Questionnaire. They are (1) Sexual Consciousness (SC), (2) Sexual Monitoring (SM), (3) Sexual Assertiveness (SA), and (4) Sex Appeal Consciousness (SAC). To find your score for each subscale, simply add the values of your responses. The items that belong to each subscale are as follows:

SC	SM	SA	SAC
1	2	3	8
4	5	6*	11
10	14	9*	29
13	17	12	
22	23*	15	
25	28	18	
	31*	30*	
	32*		

* The items marked with an asterisk should be reverse scored (i.e., 1 = 5, 2 = 4, 3 = 3, 4 = 2, and 5 = 1).

How Do You Compare?

SC		SM		SA		SAC		
M	F	M	F	M	F	M	F	PERCENTILE
27	28	32	32	26	26	11	12	85
25	26	30	29	22	22	10	10	70
23	23	27	26	17	17	9	9	50
21	20	24	23	12	12	8	8	30
19	18	22	20	8	8	7	6	15

High scores indicate higher levels of the characteristic in question. If, for instance, you had a percentile score of 70 on SM, it means that 70 percent of people scored lower than you did in Sexual Monitoring.

For more information, see William E. Snell Jr., Terri D. Fisher, and Rowland S. Miller, "Development of the Sexual Awareness Questionnaire: Components, Reliability, and Validity," *Annals of Sex Research* 4 (1991): 65–92.

ABOUT THE SEXUAL AWARENESS QUESTIONNAIRE

One relatively new development among scientists interested in human sexuality is the study of our relevant thoughts and attitudes—or cognitions, as psychologists call them. Psychologists have studied sexual behavior and emotions for more than a century, dating back to Sigmund Freud and Havelock Ellis. But it was not until the early 1990s, when William Snell, along with his colleagues Terri Fisher and Rowland Miller, published the Sexual Awareness Questionnaire that researchers had a vehicle for measuring cognitions that might influence the ways in which we express our sexuality. The Sexual Awareness Questionnaire is comprised of four subscales: Sexual Consciousness, Sexual Monitoring, Sex Appeal Consciousness, and Sexual Assertiveness.

Sexual Consciousness refers to the degree to which people are aware of their internal, private bodily sensations that portend sexual arousal and motivation. People who score high on this scale are sensitive to changes in their bodily state that reflect concupiscence, and they readily acknowledge their sexual tastes and preferences. Although this may sound like something men are particularly good at, Snell found that men and women had virtually identical scores on this scale. High scoring men and women felt good about their sexuality, and they reported a satisfying sexual relationship with their partners. There was only a very slight tendency for these people to report more general satisfaction with their relationships. Interestingly, scores on this scale do not bear any relation to the permissiveness of one's sexual attitudes, but they do correlate with the belief that one should practice safe sex.

The Sexual Monitoring subscale measures the tendency to be concerned with what others are thinking of our sexuality. People who receive high scores on this scale frequently wonder if others think they are sexually appealing and attractive. Low scorers rarely give this a thought. It simply does not occur to them to worry about how others evaluate their sex appeal. This scale provides a good example of how research results can sometimes contradict what common sense tells us. If you go back a few pages to the test itself and identify the items that appear on this scale, you would probably guess that people who score high on it tend to have problems with their self-esteem—at least, that is my guess. Several of the items include the notion of experiencing concern or worry about what others think of one's sexual appeal. But the results clearly showed that there was no relation between Sexual Monitoring and either general self-esteem or Sexual Esteem. Snell also found that scores on the Sexual-Monitoring subscale were not correlated with either sexual or relationship satisfaction. These people did, however, experience less sexual anxiety but greater sexual preoccupation than their low-scoring peers. It would seem that sexual monitors are relatively well-adjusted people who have this one, relatively isolated quirk of worrying too much about what others think of their sex appeal.

The third subscale, Sex Appeal Consciousness, is another curious scale that seems to defy common sense—or at least, my common sense. The scale, typified by Item 8, "I know when others think I'm sexy," suggests to me an individual who has a little too much confidence in his or her sex appeal. I have known people, both men and women, who are quick to point out how attracted others are to them. I am reminded of a *Seinfeld* episode in which a woman stops just short of telling George what a creep he is and later, when George is telling Jerry about the encounter, he describes it as evidence that she is interested in going out with him. Perhaps it is because I cannot remember ever having the feeling that "others think I'm sexy" that I'm a little suspicious of anyone who could say "very characteristic of me" in response to such an item. But enough of that. Let's talk about the evidence.

Snell found that people high in Sex Appeal Consciousness, compared with their low-scoring peers, were lower in sex anxiety and guilt and higher in sexual assertiveness and sexual preoccupation. Contrary to my strong expectation, there was no evidence that those high in Sex Appeal Consciousness had narcissistic tendencies, much less unusually high self-esteem or even high sexual esteem. Once again, the evidence is that high scorers are not much different from anyone else. They are a little more obsessed with sex than others, but they seem to be a basically well-adjusted group. On the other side of the coin, those with low scores on this subscale are slightly more anxious about sex and somewhat less likely to make their sexual desires known. They, too, are essentially a well-adjusted group of people.

Last, but certainly not least, is the Sexual Assertiveness subscale. As the term suggests, people in this category are not the type to passively hope that their partners will know what they like. The sexually assertive person speaks up. This person believes he or she has a right to sexual fulfillment and is not afraid to ask a partner to do what it takes to get it. This was the only one of the four subscales on the Sexual Awareness Questionnaire for which the evidence showed a clear-cut advantage to being a high scorer. Such individuals had high sexual esteem, were satisfied with their sexual relationships with their partners, and had low levels of sexual anxiety, sexual guilt, and anxiety regarding heterosexual interactions.

This also was the only one of the four scales for which there was a significant difference between men and women, with—you guessed it—men scoring higher than women. It sometimes surprises me that so little has changed in the thirty years since the so-called sexual revolution of the late 1960s and early 1970s. For those of you old enough to remember, this was the time when many women began to discard the old stereotypes that linked "good women" with purity and chastity. Women, we were told, had just as much right to sexual fulfillment as did men. Now, three decades later, substantial numbers of women continue to believe that it is not quite proper to explicitly express their sexual desires and preferences. Ironically, surveys continue to find that the number one complaint men have about women as sex partners is that they are not assertive enough. Most men appreciate women who are not afraid to let it be known when they are interested in a man. They appreciate women who share the responsibility for initiating sex. And they appreciate women who make it clear what their partner can do for them to make the sexual encounter gratifying.

Despite my initial stereotypes, after digesting Snell's statistical analysis, I believe the first three scales on his Sexual Awareness Questionnaire reflect interesting sexually related perceptions and cognitions, but scores on these scales have relatively few implications for overall adjustment. Sexual Assertiveness, however, is clearly different. The evidence is strong that people who are sexually assertive have more satisfying sexual relationships. So, if you did receive a low score on this scale, you might find it gratifying to speak up, to let your partner know what you are thinking and what you want when it comes to sex. Both you and your partner will be happier for it.

CHAPTER FIFTEEN

The Multidimensional Sexuality Questionnaire

The following statements concern the topic of sexual relationships. Please read each item carefully, and decide to what extent it is characteristic of you. Some of the items refer to a specific sexual relationship. Whenever possible, answer the questions with your most recent partner in mind. If you have never had a sexual relationship, answer in terms of what you think your responses would most likely be. Then, for each statement, fill in the response in the blank before each item that indicates how much it applies to you by using the following scale:

1 = Not at all characteristic of me
2 = Slightly characteristic of me
3 = Somewhat characteristic of me
4 = Moderately characteristic of me
5 = Very characteristic of me

* Reprinted with permission of Dr. William E. Snell Jr., Southeast Missouri State University, Cape Girardeau, Missouri.

____ 1. My sexuality is something that I am largely responsible for.

____ 2. I am very motivated to be sexually active.

____ 3. I feel anxious when I think about the sexual aspects of my life.

____ 4. The sexual aspects of my life are determined mostly by chance happenings.

____ 5. I am somewhat afraid of becoming sexually involved with another person.

____ 6. I am very satisfied with the way my sexual needs are currently being met.

____ 7. The sexual aspects of my life are determined in large part by my own behavior.

____ 8. I am strongly motivated to devote time and effort to sex.

____ 9. I am worried about the sexual aspects of my life.

____ 10. Most things that affect the sexual aspects of my life happen to me by accident.

____ 11. I sometimes have a fear of sexual relationships.

____ 12. I am very satisfied with my sexual relationship.

____ 13. I am in control of the sexual aspects of my life.

____ 14. I have a strong desire to be sexually active.

____ 15. Thinking about the sexual aspects of my life leaves me with an uneasy feeling.

____ 16. Luck plays a big part in influencing the sexual aspects of my life.

____ 17. I sometimes am fearful of sexual activity.

---

1 = Not at all characteristic of me; 2 = Slightly characteristic of me;
3 = Somewhat characteristic of me;
4 = Moderately characteristic of me; 5 = Very characteristic of me

___ 18. My sexual relationship meets my original expectations.

___ 19. The main thing that affects the sexual aspects of my life is what I myself do.

___ 20. It's really important to me that I involve myself in sexual activity.

___ 21. I usually worry about the sexual aspects of my life.

___ 22. The sexual aspects of my life are largely a matter of (good or bad) fortune.

___ 23. I don't have very much fear about engaging in sex.

___ 24. My sexual relationship is very good compared with most.

___ 25. My sexuality is something that I myself am in charge of.

___ 26. I strive to keep myself sexually active.

___ 27. I feel nervous when I think about the sexual aspects of my life.

___ 28. The sexual aspects of my life are a matter of fate (destiny).

___ 29. I'm not very afraid of becoming sexually active.

___ 30. I am very satisfied with the sexual aspects of my life.

---

1 = Not at all characteristic of me; 2 = Slightly characteristic of me;
3 = Somewhat characteristic of me;
4 = Moderately characteristic of me; 5 = Very characteristic of me

Scoring

There are six subscales to the Multidimensional Sexuality Questionnaire. They are (1) Internal Sexual Control (ISC), (2) Sexual Motivation (SM), (3) Sexual Anxiety (SA), (4) External Sexual Control (ESC), (5) Fear of Sexual Relationships (FSR), and (6) Sexual Satisfaction (SS). To find your score for each subscale, simply add the values of your responses. The items that belong to each subscale are as follows:

ISC	SM	SA	ESC	FSR	SS
1	2	3	4	5	6
7	8	9	10	11	12
13	14	15	16	17	18
19	20	21	22	23	24
25	26	27	28	29	30

How Do You Compare?

ISC		SM		SA		ESC		FSR		SS		Percentile
M	F	M	F	M	F	M	F	M	F	M	F	
18	18	17	13	11	10	9	6	12	14	18	18	85
16	16	15	11	9	8	7	5	10	12	16	16	70
13	13	12	8	6	5	5	3	7	9	13	13	50
10	10	9	5	3	2	3	1	4	6	10	10	30
8	8	7	3	1	0	1	0	2	4	8	8	15

High scores indicate higher levels of the characteristic in question. If, for instance, you received a percentile score of 70 on SA, it means that 70 percent of people have less Sexual Anxiety than do you.

For more information, see William E. Snell Jr., Terri D. Fisher, and Andrew S. Walters, "The Multidimensional

Sexuality Questionnaire: An Objective Self-Report Measure of Psychological Tendencies Associated with Human Sexuality," *Annals of Sex Research* 6 (1993): 27–55.

ABOUT THE MULTIDIMENSIONAL SEXUALITY QUESTIONNAIRE

The Multidimensional Sexuality Questionnaire (MSQ) represents a third stage in Snell's attempt to provide a comprehensive instrument to measure a variety of elements of human sexuality. This test consists of twelve scales, six of which appeared on one of his first two tests presented in Part III. I have included only the six new scales here because there would be little point to your taking the same test twice. Let us take a look at these six new scales and what they measure.

The first scale is called Internal Sexual Control. It represents the belief that one has personal control over the sexual aspects of one's life. People who believe they have personal control are more likely to take an active role in influencing the kinds of sexual experiences they have. The sexual behavior of these people is not much different from people in general; for instance, they are no more or no less permissive than the average person. They are, however, more sexually assertive, have less sexual anxiety, have higher sexual esteem, and experience greater sexual satisfaction in their relationships. Overall, it appears to be "good" to have a high score on this scale.

On the second scale, which measures Sexual Motivation, men received considerably higher scores than did women. As you might guess, both men and women with high scores on this scale have active and satisfying sex lives. High scorers are likely to have had numerous sexual partners, and they do not see the point in waiting very long after meeting a potential partner to have sex. Furthermore, they do not view love as an essential requirement for sexual relationships, and consequently, they are likely to have casual sexual relationships. Clearly, these people have a rather permissive view of sex—a view that I would argue is neither inherently good nor bad. But it is important that partners have similar scores on this scale. A relationship between a low scorer and a high scorer might produce more than its share of misunderstandings and hurt feelings.

Sexual Anxiety is the third scale on the MSQ. People with sexual anxiety tend to be concerned that others will disapprove of or even punish them for any expression of their sexuality. This makes it difficult for people high in sexual anxiety to initiate sexual relationships and may even limit the sexual activities they engage in with a regular partner. Although these people are just as interested in sex as anyone else, their anxiety makes it difficult for them to have the kinds of sexual experiences they would like. Consequently, they tend to be sexually depressed.

Sexual anxiety is more likely to be a problem for men than for women because men still bear most of the onus of initiating sexual relationships. In extreme cases, such men may find it nearly impossible to make the first move in a relationship, even when the woman is trying her hardest to signal that she's receptive. In the absence of explicit instructions to the contrary, they worry that the woman will chastise them if they make a sexual overture. In milder cases, the men are capable of introducing sex into a relationship; they simply need more proof than the average man that the woman is interested. If you had an extremely high score on this scale, you may be able to reduce your level of anxiety with the help of an understanding and supportive partner.

On the next scale, External Sexual Control, surprisingly (at least to me), men had higher scores than did women. People with high scores on this scale tend to believe that their sex lives are largely a matter of chance or fate; they feel they have little control as to the kinds of sexual experiences they have. It is surprising that men are more likely to hold this view than women because men are clearly more sexually assertive than their fairer counterparts. And assertive people tend to get what they want. Perhaps women receive lower scores on this scale (despite three decades of railing against the double standard) because they have the power of saying yes or no. Despite three decades of talking about sexual equality, men still do most of the asking, and women mostly wait to be asked. Men, even when they are assertive, may feel that whether a woman says yes or no is a matter of luck or fate. Yes, men must take the initiative if they are to find a sex partner, but in the end, they are at the mercy of the woman, who is firmly established in her role as the gatekeeper of sexual contact.

The fifth scale on the MSQ is Fear of Sexual Relationships. Although women did score significantly higher on this scale than did men, the average scores for both men and women were very low. Clearly, an outright fear of having a sexual relationship is relatively rare. Those few people who did have high scores on this scale had high levels of sexual anxiety and sexual depression. Also, they had low levels of sexual esteem, sexual assertiveness, and sexual satisfaction. This is one scale with very serious implications. There are people who are so frightened of the possibility of having a sexual encounter that they will avoid any kind of relationship with the other sex. They live with the fear that befriending someone might lead to an expectation of sex. Also, some people are so worried about their perceived sexual inadequacies that they avoid forming sexual relationships for fear that their inadequacies might be revealed. More common in women, this fear sometimes results from a history of childhood sexual abuse. If you or your partner received a very high score on this scale, it is important to know that you do not have to continue to live with the fear. This is a condition that responds well to psychotherapy, and I urge you to find a competent therapist right away. It is possible for you to have a much more gratifying life.

The final scale on the MSQ is Sexual Satisfaction. This scale provides a good yardstick for comparing yourself with others, but more importantly, it can serve as a check as to whether you and your partner view your relationship in similar ways. One of the perplexing things about sex is that it is often harder for people to talk about it than to do it. So it is not unusual for one partner to feel somewhat dissatisfied with the relationship and not express those feelings directly. I've seen many of these couples in therapy, and the satisfied partner (more often than not the man) inevitably asks, "Why didn't you tell me?" The answer is usually a rather weak, "I tried to," but the trying typically consisted of hints so subtle that it would take a clairvoyant to detect the message. The obvious point is that if you and your partner have considerably different scores on this scale, you should talk about your perspectives. Sex rarely gets better on its own, so if you are to have any chance of having a relationship that is satisfying for both of you, you must talk about your feelings and be explicit about what you would like to see changed.

CHAPTER SIXTEEN

The Multidimensional Sexual Self-Concept Questionnaire

The items in this questionnaire refer to people's sexuality. Please read each item carefully and decide to what extent it is characteristic of you. Give each item a rating of how much it applies to you by using the following scale. (Remember to respond to all items, even if you are not completely sure.)

1 = Not at all characteristic of me
2 = Slightly characteristic of me
3 = Somewhat characteristic of me
4 = Moderately characteristic of me
5 = Very characteristic of me

---

* Reprinted with permission of Dr. William E. Snell Jr., Southeast Missouri State University, Cape Girardeau, Missouri.

___ 1. I have the ability to take care of any sexual needs and desires that I may have.

___ 2. I am very aware of my sexual feelings and needs.

___ 3. I am motivated to avoid engaging in "risky" (i.e., unprotected) sexual behavior.

___ 4. I expect that the sexual aspects of my life will be positive and rewarding in the future.

___ 5. I would be to blame if the sexual aspects of my life were not going very well.

___ 6. If I were to experience a sexual problem, I myself would be in control of whether this improved.

___ 7. My sexual behaviors are determined largely by other more powerful and influential individuals.

___ 8. Not only would I be a good sexual partner, but it's quite important to me that I be a good sexual partner.

___ 9. If I am careful, then I will be able to prevent myself from having any sexual problems.

___ 10. I am competent enough to make sure that my sexual needs are fulfilled.

___ 11. I am very aware of my sexual motivations and desires.

___ 12. I am motivated to keep myself from having any "risky" sexual behavior (e.g., exposure to sexual diseases).

___ 13. I believe that in the future, the sexual aspects of my life will be healthy and positive.

___ 14. If the sexual aspects of my life were to go wrong, I would be the person to blame.

___ 15. If I were to experience a sexual problem, my own behavior would determine whether I improved.

---

1 = Not at all characteristic of me; 2 = Slightly characteristic of me;
3 = Somewhat characteristic of me;
4 = Moderately characteristic of me; 5 = Very characteristic of me

___ 16. My sexual behaviors are largely controlled by people other than myself (e.g., my partner, friends, and family).

___ 17. Not only would I be a skilled sexual partner, but it's very important to me that I be a skilled sexual partner.

___ 18. I can pretty much prevent myself from developing sexual problems by taking good care of myself.

___ 19. I have the skills and ability to ensure rewarding sexual behaviors for myself.

___ 20. I tend to think about my own sexual beliefs and attitudes.

___ 21. I want to avoid engaging in sex where I might be exposed to sexual diseases.

___ 22. I do not expect to suffer any sexual problems or frustrations in the future.

___ 23. If I were to develop a sexual disorder, then I would be to blame for not taking good care of myself.

___ 24. If I were to become sexually maladjusted, I myself would be responsible for making myself better.

___ 25. My sexual behavior is determined by the actions of powerful others (e.g., my partner, friends, and family).

___ 26. Not only could I relate well to a sexual partner, but it's important to me that I be able to do so.

___ 27. If I look out for myself, then I will be able to avoid any sexual problems in the future.

___ 28. I am able to cope with and to handle my own sexual needs and wants.

___ 29. I'm very alert to changes in my sexual thoughts, feelings, and desires.

___ 30. I really want to prevent myself from being exposed to sexual diseases.

---

1 = Not at all characteristic of me; 2 = Slightly characteristic of me;
3 = Somewhat characteristic of me;
4 = Moderately characteristic of me; 5 = Very characteristic of me

___ 31. I will probably experience some sexual problems in the future.

___ 32. If I were to develop a sexual problem, then it would be my own fault for letting it happen.

___ 33. If I developed any sexual problems, my recovery would depend in large part on what I myself would do.

___ 34. In order to be sexually active, I have to conform to other, more powerful, individuals.

___ 35. I am able to "connect" well with a sexual partner, and it's important to me that I am able to do so.

___ 36. I will be able to avoid any sexual problems if I just take good care of myself.

___ 37. I have the capability to take care of my own sexual needs and desires.

___ 38. I am very aware of the sexual aspects of myself (e.g., habits, thoughts, and beliefs).

___ 39. I am really motivated to avoid any sexual activity that might expose me to sexual diseases.

___ 40. I anticipate that in the future, the sexual aspects of my life will be frustrating.

___ 41. If something went wrong with my own sexuality, then it would be my own fault.

___ 42. If I developed a sexual disorder, my recovery would depend on how I myself dealt with the problem.

___ 43. My sexual behavior is mostly determined by people who have influence and control over me.

___ 44. Not only am I capable of relating to a sexual partner, but it's important to me that I relate very well.

___ 45. If I just pay careful attention, I'll be able to prevent myself from having any sexual problems.

---

1 = Not at all characteristic of me; 2 = Slightly characteristic of me;
3 = Somewhat characteristic of me;
4 = Moderately characteristic of me; 5 = Very characteristic of me

SCORING

There are eight subscales to the Multidimensional Sexual Self-Concept Questionnaire. They are (1) Sexual Self-Efficacy (SSE), (2) Motivation to Avoid Risky Sex (MARS), (3) Sexual Optimism (SO), (4) Sexual Problem Self-Blame (SPSB), (5) Sexual Problem Management (SPM), (6) Powerful Other Sexual Control (POSC), (7) Sexual Self-Schema (SSS), and (8) Sexual Problem Prevention (SPP). To find your score for each subscale, simply add the values of your responses. The items that belong to each subscale are as follows:

SSE	MARS	SO	SPSB	SPM	POSC	SSS	SPP
1	3	4	5	6	7	8	9
10	12	13	14	15	16	17	18
19	21	22	23	24	25	26	27
28	30	31*	32	33	34	35	36
37	39	40*	41	42	43	44	45

* The two items marked with an asterisk (31 and 40) should be reverse scored (i.e., 1 = 5, 2 = 4, 3 = 3, 4 = 2, and 5 = 1).

HOW DO YOU COMPARE?

SSE		MARS		SO		SPSB		SPM		POSC		SSS		SPP		
M	F	M	F	M	F	M	F	M	F	M	F	M	F	M	F	PERCENTILE
23	23	25	26	22	24	20	20	22	22	13	13	25	24	22	22	85
21	20	23	24	20	22	18	18	20	20	11	11	23	22	20	20	70
19	18	21	23	19	20	16	15	18	18	9	9	21	20	18	17	50
17	16	19	22	18	18	14	12	16	16	7	7	19	18	16	14	30
15	13	17	20	16	16	12	10	14	14	5	5	17	16	14	12	15

High scores indicate higher levels of the characteristic in question. If, for instance, you received a percentile score of 70 on SO, it means that 70 percent of people have less Sexual Optimism than do you.

For more information, see William E. Snell Jr., "Measuring Multiple Aspects of the Sexual Self-Concept: The Multidimensional Sexual Self-Concept Questionnaire," unpublished manuscript. Department of Psychology, Southeast Missouri State University, Cape Girardeau, Missouri, 1996.

ABOUT THE MULTIDIMENSIONAL SEXUAL SELF-CONCEPT QUESTIONNAIRE

Psychologist William Snell has continued his quest to measure most every conceivable aspect of sexuality. He revised several of the scales on his Multidimensional Sexuality Questionnaire and developed nine completely new subscales to comprise his most recent test, the Multidimensional Sexual Self-Concept Questionnaire (MSSQ). Along with publishing information about the technical qualities of the instrument, Snell collected a good deal of additional information that makes it possible to have a more complete picture of the meaning of the scores on the various scales. Let us take a look at his findings. (Incidentally, presented here is an abbreviated version of the original questionnaire; you learned about twelve of the twenty scales when you completed the preceding three tests.)

First is the Sexual Self-Efficacy scale. As you can see from the items that appear on this scale, people with high scores have confidence in their ability to satisfy their sexual needs and desires. Interestingly, men and women had very similar scores on this scale. Both men and women who receive high scores on this scale have positive feelings about their sexuality, and they tend to experience high levels of satisfaction with the sexual side of their relationship.

As part of his research with this test, Snell examined the correspondence between its scales and attachment style. Attachment style has been a popular topic among researchers over the past decade. The theory is that the type of attachment one experiences as a child will have important implications for adult romantic relationships. At least four basic types of attachment styles have been proposed: secure, preoccupied, fearful, and dismissive. The relationships of men and women with high levels of sexual self-efficacy tend to be characterized as secure. They feel good about their roles in the relationships, and they expect their partners will be equally trustworthy, accepting, and responsive. These people view their relationships as important and feel a clear sense of commitment to them. Curiously, a high score on this scale predicts a tendency for men, but not women, to believe that after first meeting someone, it is wise to wait longer to have sex.

The name of the second scale, Motivation to Avoid Risky Sex, says it all. Such people are concerned about sexually transmitted diseases and, consequently, are more likely to have used condoms in both their first and in their most recent sexual encounters. A number of researchers have found that when it comes to safe sex, most people talk the talk, but a significant minority fail to walk the walk. The typical advice offered by experts is to talk with prospective sexual partners about your respective sexual histories, but you should bear in mind that as many as one third of men and one fourth of women admit having lied to a prospective partner. It is certainly a good sign if your partner has a high score on this scale, but I would still recommend that you go together to be tested for sexually transmitted diseases before initiating a sexual relationship.

Sexual Optimism, the third scale, was highly correlated with the Sexual Self-Efficacy scale. Men and women had nearly identical scores on this scale, and they both expected to have satisfying sexual relationships in the future. They tended to have a secure attachment with their partners, felt a sense of commitment toward their relationships, and found it both satisfying and important.

Three of the scales on the questionnaire, the Sexual Problem Self-Blame, the Sexual Problem Management, and the Sexual Problem Prevention scales, measured beliefs about one's role in and one's ability to deal with potential sexual problems. There were no surprises regarding these scales, with one exception: women, but not men, who accepted the blame for sexual problems in a relationship and who felt capable of preventing such problems in the future were somewhat more likely to have had numerous casual sexual relationships. Perhaps their experiences provided them with a basis for believing they could deal effectively with such problems.

Incidentally, the two most common causes of sexual problems are performance anxiety and poor communication between the partners. Consider the following scenario, one that is all too familiar to sex therapists. John has a problem with premature ejaculation. He knows his partner was frustrated by their last encounter, but he vows to try harder the next time. Susan was understanding at first, certain that it would get better with time. But her patience has run out. She believes that John is simply selfish and has begun to avoid having sex with him to avoid being disappointed again. John approaches their next encounter more anxious than ever, and this, taken together with their not having had sex for several weeks, results in John having his orgasm quicker than ever before. John is humiliated. Susan is both frustrated and angry. They both roll over and pretend to fall asleep.

The solution to the problem is obvious. If John shares his feelings of anxiety with Susan, she will have reason to be more patient. If Susan tells John of her frustration, they may think of ways to ensure that Susan is not left hanging after every encounter. There is a good chance that this alone will reduce John's anxiety to the point where he can develop a pattern more satisfying for both him and Susan. If not, the two of them could consult self-help books and, if necessary, a therapist. Indeed, the only way their problem can continue or become more severe is for them to grit their teeth, keep their feelings to themselves, and hope that things will get better. Life is too short to give hope a free rein.

The next scale is called the Powerful Other Sexual Control scale. People who score high on this scale believe that their sexual behavior is influenced by other people, more powerful than themselves. The belief that one's fate in general is influenced by powerful others has been researched extensively, and Snell was interested in whether this had implications for one's sexuality. As you can tell from the normative tables, most people do not believe that powerful others have much effect on their sexuality, but there is one disturbing exception. Snell found evidence that women who received high scores on this scale were somewhat likely to have had their first sexual experience, an abusive and strongly negative one, with a family member or relative. It makes sense that women who were the victims of sexual abuse as children would come to view powerful others as controlling the expression of their sexuality. For men, this relationship did not hold. However, men who scored high on this scale did report more sexual anxiety, sexual depression, and sexual fear. One cannot help but wonder if they too were the victims of some "powerful other" but chose not to report it.

Finally, there is the Sexual Self-Schema scale. People with high scores on this scale believe they are good sexual partners, and it is quite important to them that they be perceived that way. Despite the popular stereotype (held mostly by women) that men need to think of themselves as great lovers, women's scores on this scale were not significantly different from men's scores.

Women with high scores on this scale tended to have high sexual motivation and experienced high levels of sexual satisfaction. They were likely to have had numerous sexual partners, they did not believe it was necessary to be in love with someone before having sex with him, and they saw no reason not to have sex with a man shortly after meeting him. The results for men were not as clear, but high-scoring men were actually lower than average in sexual preoccupation. They rated their current sexual relationship as quite important, but they did not anticipate it would last long.

As always, it is important to keep in mind that psychological tests can be quite effective when predicting the behavior for large groups of people, but there is lots of room for error when making predictions for any particular individual. So, if we had a group of one hundred men all of whom had high scores on the Sexual Self-Schema scale, it would be safe to bet that on average, they would expect their current relationships to be short-lived. But it would not be a very good bet to make the same prediction for one specific man who received a high score on this scale. If your partner received a high score on this scale, you should not take it as proof that she has had an extensive sexual history or that he expects your relationship to end any day now.

CHAPTER SEVENTEEN

The Sexual Relationship Scale

The statements in this scale concern the topic of sexual relationships. Please read each of the statements carefully, and decide to what extent it is characteristic of you. Some of the items refer to a specific relationship. Whenever possible, answer the questions with your current partner in mind. If you are not currently dating anyone, answer the questions with your most recent partner in mind. If you have never had a relationship, answer in terms of what you think your responses would most likely be. Then, for each statement, fill in the response in the blank that indicates how much it applies to you by using the following scale. (Remember to respond to all items, even if you are not completely sure.)

1 = Not at all characteristic of me
2 = Slightly characteristic of me
3 = Somewhat characteristic of me
4 = Moderately characteristic of me
5 = Very characteristic of me

* Reprinted with permission of Dr. William E. Snell Jr., Southeast Missouri State University, Cape Girardeau, Missouri.

___ 1. It would bother me if my sexual partner neglected my needs.

___ 2. When I make love with someone, I generally expect something in return.

___ 3. If I were to make love with a sexual partner, I'd take that person's needs and feelings into account.

___ 4. If a sexual partner were to do something sensual for me, I'd try to do the same for him/her.

___ 5. I'm not especially sensitive to the feelings of a sexual partner.

___ 6. I don't think people should feel obligated to repay an intimate partner for sexual favors.

___ 7. I don't consider myself to be a particularly helpful sexual partner.

___ 8. I wouldn't feel all that exploited if an intimate partner failed to repay me for a sexual favor.

___ 9. I believe sexual lovers should go out of their way to be sexually responsive to their partners.

___ 10. I wouldn't bother to keep track of the times a sexual partner asked for a sensual pleasure.

___ 11. I wouldn't especially enjoy helping a partner achieve his/her own sexual satisfaction.

___ 12. When a person receives sexual pleasures from another, she/he ought to repay that person right away.

___ 13. I expect a sexual partner to be responsive to my sexual needs and feelings.

---

1 = Not at all characteristic of me; 2 = Slightly characteristic of me;
3 = Somewhat characteristic of me;
4 = Moderately characteristic of me; 5 = Very characteristic of me

___ 14. It's best to make sure things are always kept "even" between two people in a sexual relationship.

___ 15. I would be willing to go out of my way to satisfy my sexual partner.

___ 16. I would do a special sexual favor for an intimate partner only if that person did some special sexual favor for me.

___ 17. I don't think it's wise to get involved taking care of a partner's sexual needs.

___ 18. If my sexual partner performed a sexual request for me, I wouldn't feel that I'd have to repay him/her later on.

___ 19. I'm not the sort of person who would help a partner with a sexual problem.

___ 20. If my sexual partner wanted something special from me, she/he would have to so something sexual for me.

___ 21. If I were feeling sexually needy, I'd ask my sexual partner for help.

___ 22. If my sexual partner became emotionally upset, I would try to avoid him/her.

___ 23. People should keep their sexual problems to themselves.

___ 24. If a sexual partner were to ignore my sexual needs, I'd feel hurt.

1 = Not at all characteristic of me; 2 = Slightly characteristic of me;
3 = Somewhat characteristic of me;
4 = Moderately characteristic of me; 5 = Very characteristic of me

SCORING

The Sexual Relationship Scale consists of two subscales. They are (1) the Exchange Approach to Sexual Relations (EA) and (2) the Communal Approach to Sexual Relations (CA). Each consists of eight separate items. Simply add together your responses to obtain your score on each scale. The items belonging to each subscale are as follows:

EA	CA
2	1
6*	3
8*	4
10*	9
12	13
14	15
16	21
18*	24

* The items marked with an asterisk (Items 6, 8, 10, and 18) are reversed scored (i.e., 1 = 5, 2 = 4, 3 = 3, 4 = 2, and 5 = 1).

HOW DO YOU COMPARE?

EA		CA		
F	M	F	M	Percentile
17	19	30	29	85
14	16	28	26	70
11	14	25	24	50
9	12	22	22	30
6	9	20	19	15

High scores indicate higher levels of the quality in question. If, for example, you received a percentile score of 70 on CA, it means that 70 percent of people have less of a Communal Approach to Sexual Relations than do you.

For more information, see Thomas G. Hughes and William E. Snell Jr., "Communal and Exchange Approaches to Sexual Relations," *Annals of Sex Research* 3 (1990): 149–163.

ABOUT THE SEXUAL RELATIONSHIP SCALE

Psychologist Margaret Clark suggested that intimate relationships could be categorized in one of two ways. A communal relationship is characterized by the partners' concern for each other's welfare. Each gives freely of himself or herself, confident that the other is equally trustworthy, loving, and giving. Men and women in an exchange relationship, on the other hand, feel no special obligation to take on the responsibility for the welfare or the needs of the partner. They give of themselves only when they are paying back a benefit already received or when they feel confident they will receive a benefit in return. At the risk of oversimplification, a man who tells his partner, "I know you're feeling tense. Let me massage your back," with no expectation of receiving anything in return is in a communal relationship. The man who says, "I'll massage your back if you rub my feet," is in an exchange relationship.

This distinction was found to have important implications. We tend to have exchange relationships with acquaintances, casual friends, and business associates, but our intimate relationships are usually communal. Indeed, it has been found that people whose intimate relationships are best characterized as exchange are likely to feel exploited, manipulated, and dissatisfied.

Thomas Hughes, a student of William Snell's, believed that this distinction could be extended to sexual relationships. So, under the tutelage of Snell, he constructed the Sexual Relations Scale to measure the communal and exchange approaches to sex. Surprisingly, Hughes and Snell found that these two approaches were not mutually exclusive. Although some men and women were high on one scale and low on the other, a number of people were high on both scales or low on both scales. Interestingly, men and women had nearly identical average scores on the Sexual Communion scale, but men scored significantly higher on the Sexual Exchange scale. The authors suggested that this finding was consistent with the stereotype that men take a more businesslike approach to sex.

The authors were surprised by several of their results. First, there was only a modest tendency for people's orientation toward sexual relationships to correspond to their orientation to their overall relationships. There were several men and women who had a communal approach to their relationship but an exchange approach to their sexual encounters. The converse was also true.

Second, there was only a slight tendency for sexual orientation to predict relationship satisfaction. As Hughes and Snell predicted, men who had an exchange orientation to sex were less satisfied with their relationships, and women who had a communal orientation were more satisfied. However, the test scores of women with an exchange orientation and those of men with a communal orientation had no correspondence with satisfaction with their relationships.

I am not as surprised by the failure to find a correspondence between sexual relationship orientation and sexual satisfaction. I admit that a communal approach is the ideal, but I suspect it is often a rather elusive ideal. It would be nice if people could experience the peaks of ecstasy when they thought only of their partners' satisfaction, but the reality is that men and women have somewhat different sexual needs. This makes it unlikely that one is going to get exactly what he or she wants if one is only concerned about the partner's gratification.

Countless studies have found that the number one complaint that women have about their sexual encounters is that there is too little emotional intimacy and too little foreplay. The number one complaint of men is that their partners are not sexually aggressive enough. The old cliché about men wanting to have sex and women wanting to make love has achieved the status of cliché because it has a large grain of truth to it.

A majority of sex therapists explicitly advocate an exchange approach to sexual encounters. Gender differences aside, there is enough variability in sexual tastes and preferences that it is unlikely that either men or women will be satisfied over the long run unless their partners are willing to engage in certain activities solely for their benefit. And if the partners are diligent in ensuring that the exchange of sexual favors is fair, their sexual relationships can become almost communal in nature. Consider the case of Judy and Doug.

"Doug likes to have fast vigorous sex at any time of the day or night. He might get turned on when I'm drying myself from a shower, and within two minutes it's all over with. I enjoyed it at first, but I missed the cuddling and caressing that we used to do for hours while we were dating. Finally, I reached the point where I resented his style so much, I couldn't respond to it at all.

"We finally saw a therapist, and she suggested that we try a 'take turns' approach. For every quickie, Doug had to devote an hour to making sure that I got what I wanted. It worked out great. When Doug saw how excited I became when we took our time, he couldn't help but respond to it. And once I felt confident that I would get what I wanted, I began to enjoy the quickies again because I knew how much Doug liked them."

Perhaps I'm too cynical for my own good, but I suspect that communal relationships can exist only as long as "exchanges" are made equitably. I believe that my wife, Meredith, and I have what most people would describe as a communal relationship. I know that Meredith will always be on my side, and she knows she can always count on me. But our communion is based, at least in part, on a sense of fairness about the exchanges we make. She cooks dinner, and I clean up the kitchen. She cuts the grass, and I do the edging. There have been times when our exchanges have fallen out of balance (I admit it, I'm the guilty one), and during those times, our communion clearly suffers. I do believe that people can develop the sense of having a communal relationship—which is a special feeling—as long as they ensure they are giving as many benefits as they are receiving.

CHAPTER EIGHTEEN

The Sexual Self-Disclosure Scale

Almost everyone has been in a close, intimate relationship with another person at some point in their life or plans to become involved with someone in the future. People who are involved in a close, intimate relationship have a large variety of things they can discuss with each other. This survey is concerned with the extent to which people are willing to discuss several topics about their close relationships with their intimate partners. Thus, for the disclosure topics listed in this survey, you will be asked to indicate how willing you would be to discuss these topics with an intimate partner.

* Reprinted with permission of Dr. William E. Snell Jr., Southeast Missouri State University, Cape Girardeau, Missouri.

For each of the following statements, indicate how willing you would be to discuss that topic with an intimate partner. Use the following scale:

1 = I would *not be willing* to discuss this topic with an intimate partner.

2 = I would *be slightly willing* to discuss this topic with an intimate partner.

3 = I would *be moderately willing* to discuss this topic with an intimate partner.

4 = I would *be mostly willing* to discuss this topic with an intimate partner.

5 = I would *be completely willing* to discuss this topic with an intimate partner.

___ 1. My past sexual experiences

___ 2. The kinds of touching that sexually arouse me

___ 3. My private sexual fantasies

___ 4. The sexual preferences that I have

___ 5. The types of sexual behaviors I have engaged in

___ 6. The sensations that are sexually exciting to me

___ 7. My "juicy" sexual thoughts

___ 8. What I would desire in a sexual encounter

___ 9. The sexual positions I have tried

___ 10. The types of sexual foreplay that feel arousing to me

___ 11. The sexual episodes that I daydream about

___ 12. The things I enjoy most about sex

___ 13. What sex in an intimate relationship means to me

___ 14. My private beliefs about sexual responsibility

___ 15. Times when sex was distressing for me

___ 16. The times I have pretended to enjoy sex

___ 17. Times when I prefer to refrain from sexual activity

___ 18. What it means to me to have sex with my partner

___ 19. My own ideas about sexual accountability

___ 20. Times when I was pressured to have sex

___ 21. The times I have lied about sexual matters

___ 22. The times when I might not want to have sex

___ 23. What I think and feel about having sex with my partner

___ 24. The notion that one is accountable for one's sexual behaviors

---

1 = Not be willing; 2 = Be slightly willing; 3 = Be moderately willing;
4 = Be mostly willing; 5 = Be completely willing

___ 25. The aspects of sex that bother me

___ 26. How I would feel about sexual dishonesty

___ 27. My ideas about not having sex unless I want to

___ 28. How I feel about abortions

___ 29. My personal views about homosexuals

___ 30. My own ideas about why rapes occur

___ 31. My personal views about people with AIDS

___ 32. What I consider "proper" sexual behavior

___ 33. My beliefs about pregnancy prevention

___ 34. Opinions I have about homosexual relationships

___ 35. What I really feel about rape

___ 36. Concerns that I have about the disease AIDS

___ 37. The sexual behaviors that I consider appropriate

___ 38. How I feel about pregnancy at this time

___ 39. My reactions to working with a homosexual

___ 40. My reactions to rape

___ 41. My feelings about working with someone who has AIDS

___ 42. My personal beliefs about sexual morality

___ 43. How *satisfied* I feel about the sexual aspects of my life

___ 44. How *guilty* I feel about the sexual aspects of my life

___ 45. How *calm* I feel about the sexual aspects of my life

___ 46. How *depressed* I feel about the sexual aspects of my life

---

1 = Not be willing; 2 = Be slightly willing; 3 = Be moderately willing;
4 = Be mostly willing; 5 = Be completely willing

___ 47. How *jealous* I feel about the sexual aspects of my life

___ 48. How *apathetic* I feel about the sexual aspects of my life

___ 49. How *anxious* I feel about the sexual aspects of my life

___ 50. How *happy* I feel about the sexual aspects of my life

___ 51. How *angry* I feel about the sexual aspects of my life

___ 52. How *afraid* I feel about the sexual aspects of my life

___ 53. How *pleased* I feel about the sexual aspects of my life

___ 54. How *shameful* I feel about the sexual aspects of my life

___ 55. How *serene* I feel about the sexual aspects of my life

___ 56. How *sad* I feel about the sexual aspects of my life

___ 57. How *possessive* I feel about the sexual aspects of my life (i.e., my partner)

___ 58. How *indifferent* I feel about the sexual aspects of my life

___ 59. How *troubled* I feel about the sexual aspects of my life

___ 60. How *cheerful* I feel about the sexual aspects of my life

___ 61. How *mad* I feel about the sexual aspects of my life

___ 62. How *fearful* I feel about the sexual aspects of my life

___ 63. How *delighted* I feel about the sexual aspects of my life

___ 64. How *embarrassed* I feel about the sexual aspects of my life

___ 65. How *relaxed* I feel about the sexual aspects of my life

___ 66. How *unhappy* I feel about the sexual aspects of my life

1 = Not be willing; 2 = Be slightly willing; 3 = Be moderately willing;
4 = Be mostly willing; 5 = Be completely willing

___ 67. How *suspicious* I feel about the sexual aspects of my life

___ 68. How *detached* I feel about the sexual aspects of my life

___ 69. How *worried* I feel about the sexual aspects of my life

___ 70. How *joyful* I feel about the sexual aspects of my life

___ 71. How *irritated* I feel about the sexual aspects of my life

___ 72. How *frightened* I feel about the sexual aspects of my life

1 = Not be willing; 2 = Be slightly willing; 3 = Be moderately willing;
4 = Be mostly willing; 5 = Be completely willing

SCORING

There are four scales to the Multidimensional Sexuality Questionnaire. They are (1) Sexual Behaviors (SB), (2) Sexual Values and Preferences (SVP), (3) Sexual Attitudes (SA), and (4) Sexual Feelings and Emotions (SFE). To find your score for each subscale, simply add together the values of your responses. The items that belong to each subscale are as follows:

Sexual Behaviors	Items 1–12
Sexual Values and Preferences	Items 13–27
Sexual Attitudes	Items 28–42
Sexual Feelings and Emotions	Items 43–72

HOW DO YOU COMPARE?

SB		SVP		SA		SFE		
F	M	F	M	F	M	F	M	PERCENTILE
43	46	54	63	63	63	106	113	85
37	38	48	55	58	59	91	97	70
32	29	42	46	52	55	76	81	50
27	20	36	37	46	51	61	65	30
21	12	30	29	41	47	46	49	15

High scores indicate greater willingness to discuss the topic in question. If, for instance, you received a percentile score of 70 on SB, it means that 70 percent of people would be less willing than you are to discuss their Sexual Behavior with a partner.

For more information, see William E. Snell Jr., Sharyn S. Belk, Dennis R. Papini, and Steve Clark, "Development and Validation of the Sexual Self-Disclosure Scale," *Annals of Sex Research* 2 (1989): 307–334.

ABOUT THE SEXUAL SELF-DISCLOSURE SCALE

It is almost unheard of for psychologists to reach a consensus about any topic. Such a consensus has been achieved, however, regarding the importance of communication between sexual partners. From the authors of best-selling books advising couples as to how they can have even more exciting sexual encounters to serious researchers who have explored the causes of sexual dysfunctions, all experts, self-proclaimed and otherwise, agree that sexual partners must talk to each other if they are to have a satisfying sexual relationship.

Until recently, there was no efficient means of measuring one's willingness to discuss personal feelings about sex with a partner, but Dr. William Snell, an obviously hard-working psychologist, filled this vacuum with the Sexual Self-Disclosure Scale, which he constructed with the help of his colleagues, Sharyn Belk, Dennis Papini, and Steve Clark. Their original goal was to develop a test to measure clients' willingness to discuss sexual issues with a therapist, and later they extended the instrument so it could be used to assess one's willingness to discuss such issues with a partner.

The professional literature is filled with case histories of couples who may have been able to solve their own sexual problems without having to consult a therapist had they only talked to each other. Hank, for instance, suffered from the problem of premature ejaculation. He was a shy, awkward teenager who felt inadequate around girls his own age, so he saved his hard-earned money from his job as a bag boy at a local grocery store to purchase the services of prostitutes. The women he could afford to consult depended on rapid turnover to make a decent living, so they encouraged Hank to "get it over with" as quickly as possible. He always readily agreed because he was fearful that his furtive assignations would be discovered. Later, when he married Janis, he discovered that he was helpless to change his pattern. He knew their encounters left Janis feeling frustrated, but he could not share his anxiety or the cause of it with her. Janis was left with the feeling that he could do something about it if he really wanted to and became increasingly angry at his selfishness. Finally, she insisted they consult a therapist, and with the therapist's support, Hank was able to share his early experiences with his wife (he did not reveal that the women were prostitutes). Janis was relieved to hear there was a logical explanation for his difficulty, and she promised to help him change his pattern of response. Within two weeks, they were having sexual encounters that were not only gratifying for Janis but also much more pleasurable for Hank.

Many case histories are not nearly as dramatic as Hank's. Tricia, for instance, was sexually inexperienced when she married Carl. She knew Carl had had relationships with other women and she was worried that her inexperience would mean that she would not be able to satisfy her husband. She approached every encounter feeling tense and anxious, which, of course, meant that she failed to become excited. Carl, whose experience was more limited than Tricia had assumed, concluded that he must be doing something wrong if he could not arouse his wife. Before long, his increasing anxiety level made it difficult for him to achieve erections. They too were able to share their concerns and fears with the help of a therapist, and within a few weeks, they were busy making up for lost time. If one or both of them had talked about their anxiety early in the relationship, the odds are good that they could have saved themselves months of distress, to say nothing of the cost of consulting a therapist.

Snell and his colleagues did find some interesting patterns in the responses of their normative sample. First, to no one's surprise, both men and women were much more willing to share with a partner their positive, rather than their negative, feelings about their sexual relationship. Although understandable, this is precisely the pattern that may cause problems for couples down the road. Most sexual problems develop when one of the partners, for whatever reason, begins to have negative feelings about the relationship. If these feelings can be shared in a nonthreatening, nonaccusatory fashion, it may well preclude the development of more serious and persistent problems.

Second, there were some interesting differences between men and women in what they were willing to share. I was surprised to discover, for instance, that women showed a greater willingness than men to share their sexual fantasies as well as the kinds of activities they found especially arousing. I was even more surprised to learn that men, more so than women, were willing to share their feelings about what it meant to them to have sex and their fears about their sexual encounters. In my defense, I must point out that there could be a big difference between what men say on a test about what they are willing to tell their partners and what they actually tell their partners.

More predictably, Snell found that men were more willing to talk about their beliefs regarding topics such as abortion, homosexuality, rape, and AIDS. Men probably deserve their reputation as the opinionated sex. And also not surprising was the finding that women were less willing than men to indicate a desire to delay having sex. Despite the passage of more than thirty years since the sexual revolution of the 1960s, there are clear remnants of the double standard. It would seem that women continue to believe they have an obligation to accommodate their partner, and men have less difficulty in saying no.

If you or your partner received a low score on this test, especially on the Sexual Behaviors and Sexual Feelings and Emotions scales, it would be to your advantage to make an effort to be more open with each other. I am not one of those psychologists who believes it is necessary, or even wise, to share every single thought or experience with a partner, but the evidence is overwhelming that it is better to share too much than too little.

To illustrate my point, some couples find it exciting to share their sexual fantasies and may even enjoy acting them out. But it will serve no good purpose to share a fantasy that you have reason to believe will be upsetting to your partner. On the other hand, it is almost always a good idea to share information about the kinds of stimulation that you find most pleasurable and, if necessary, the kinds of stimulation you do not especially enjoy. I remember vividly a couple I saw in therapy who was having a variety of problems. During one session, the husband complained that he had tried to get his wife interested in sex, with his favorite technique—sticking his tongue in her ear—to no avail. At that point the wife said, "There is something I've wanted to tell you for fifteen years. I've always hated that." Her husband asked why she seemed so excited when he did it, and she responded, "I thought it would mean we could move on to something else sooner." People do have a great deal in common, but there is variability in tastes. Thus, that a former partner enjoyed a particular activity does not mean your current partner will.

Should you and your partner decide it would be helpful to be more open with each other, you can use the items on this test as a vehicle for stimulating your discussion. Simply go down the list, and take turns sharing information about each item. If you do this, you will undoubtedly learn a great deal about each other, and you may well find that your sexual relationship will move up to the next level.

PART IV

Making Love Last

After taking the tests in Part IV, you will know if you have the necessary qualities, skills, and knowledge to sustain a relationship. The following tests are included in Part IV:

CHAPTER NINETEEN

The Investment and Commitment Scales

THE INVESTMENT SCALE

Please rate each of the following statements on a scale from 1 to 7, where a 1 indicates that you would be *completely uninterested* in this activity or event and a 7 indicates that you would be *greatly interested* in this activity or event.

---

* Reprinted with permission of Dr. Mary Lund, University of California, Los Angeles, Los Angeles, California.

____ 1. Spending your free time with your partner rather than doing other things or seeing other people

____ 2. Continuing the relationship over a period of time (the total length of time you have been involved)

____ 3. Spending continuous time alone together such as on dates, weekend outings, or vacations

____ 4. Buying gifts for your partner or paying for entertainment (considering both amount and expense)

____ 5. Sharing important personal feelings, problems, and beliefs with your partner

____ 6. Revealing your sexual experiences/preferences to your partner

____ 7. Exploring sexual activities with your partner

____ 8. Sharing each other's homes by exchanging keys, keeping belongings at each other's homes, sharing a dwelling, and so forth

____ 9. Sharing material possessions such as sporting equipment, furniture, a car, or a house

____ 10. Sharing something of sentimental value with your partner such as a pet or a musical instrument (considering how important it is)

____ 11. Sharing income and expenses with your partner such as transportation costs, food costs, or having a joint bank account and shared debts

____ 12. Contributing financially to your partner or your relationship in general

____ 13. Trying to develop interests and activities in common with your partner

Scale of 1 to 7
1 = Completely uninterested; 7 = Greatly interested

___ 14. Making plans for the future such as discussing living together, getting married, or having children

___ 15. Telling your partner your true feelings about the relationship such as whether you love him or her

___ 16. Making formal agreements about your relationship such as deciding to go steady, get engaged, or get married

___ 17. Letting friends know your feelings and plans about your relationship

___ 18. Integrating your partner into your family (such as introducing them, arranging shared social activities, or revealing your feelings and plans)

___ 19. Putting effort into seeing your partner (such as traveling long distances or traveling often)

___ 20. Doing favors for or helping your partner (such as lending money or doing errands)

___ 21. Changing things about yourself to please your partner such as your habits, attitudes, or appearance

___ 22. Restricting your relationships with other potential partners such as not dating or having sex with others

___ 23. Changing your career plans or other interests to continue your relationship

___ 24. Putting effort into "making the relationship work" where there were problems

___ 25. Trying to encourage and support your partner

___ 26. Investing emotionally in your partner in general

Scale of 1 to 7
1 = Completely uninterested; 7 = Greatly interested

SCORING

To find your score on this scale, simply add the values of your responses.

HOW DO YOU COMPARE?

SCORE	PERCENTILE
155	85
144	70
134	50
124	30
113	15

High scores indicate a greater investment in a relationship. If, for instance, you received a percentile score of 70, you have invested more into your relationship than have 70 percent of other people.

THE COMMITMENT SCALE

Please answer each of the following questions by providing a number between 1 and 7 in the blank next to the item, where a 1 indicates *not at all so* and a 7 indicates *very much so*.

____ 1. How likely is it that your relationship will be permanent?

____ 2. How attracted are you to other potential partners or to a single lifestyle?

____ 3. How likely is it that you and your partner will be together six months from now?

____ 4. How much trouble would ending your relationship be to you personally?

____ 5. How attractive would a potential partner have to be for you to pursue a new relationship?

____ 6. How likely are you to pursue another relationship or single lifestyle in the future?

____ 7. How obligated do you feel to continue this relationship?

____ 8. In your opinion, how committed is your partner to this relationship?

____ 9. In your opinion, how likely is your partner to continue this relationship?

SCORING

Before calculating your score on this scale, you must first reverse your responses on two items, Items 2 and 6. To do this, perform the appropriate of the following substitutions: $1 = 7, 2 = 6, 3 = 5, 4 = 4, 5 = 3, 6 = 2$, or $7 = 1$. Then, add up your responses to find your total score.

HOW DO YOU COMPARE?

SCORE	PERCENTILE
52	85
48	70
44	50
40	30
36	15

High scores indicate a greater commitment to a relationship. If, for example, you received a percentile score of 70, your commitment to your relationship is greater than that of 70 percent of other people.

For more information, see Mary Lund, "The Development of Investment and Commitment Scales for Predicting Continuity of Personal Relationships," *Journal of Social and Personal Relationships* 2 (1985): 3–23.

ABOUT THE INVESTMENT AND COMMITMENT SCALES

What does it take to keep two people together over the long term? Social psychologists have been asking this question for the past twenty-five years, and until recently, the most common answer had to do with costs and rewards. The belief was that people weighed the benefits they derived from staying in a relationship and balanced them against the negative aspects (i.e., the costs). The primary benefit was thought to be gratification of one's feelings of love. So, the stronger the feelings of love experienced by the man and woman, the more likely the relationship was to endure. Costs could include any of the myriad negative aspects that plague all relationships from time to time—arguments about money, who will wash the dishes, how to spend free time, and so on. As long as these costs did not accumulate to the point where they outweighed the rewards, this theory suggested that the relationship would continue.

Recently, Mary Lund, a psychologist with the Family Therapy Institute of Southern California, argued that the theory that people balance benefits against costs simply does not explain the course of many relationships. As an example, she cited the person who has an emotionally intense extramarital affair complete with generous benefits but does not plan to leave an empty shell marriage despite its having few benefits and untold costs. Lund proposed a barrier model to explain how people made the decision to stay or leave a relationship. Barriers are certain obstacles to discontinuing a relationship that build up over time. These barriers keep couples together during those periods when benefits are low and costs are high. Two important barriers are investment and commitment—as measured by her tests in this chapter.

Investments accumulate over time. Early in a relationship, for instance, a man might "invest" in a bouquet of flowers. A woman may "invest" with tickets to a play. These small investments may be motivated by the desire for immediate rewards, acknowledges Lund, but they can gain momentum. Before long, people begin to invest in a relationship simply because they have developed an expectation that this process will continue. To use a bit of psychological jargon, the investment process has become functionally autonomous.

Commitment works in much the same way. At the very beginning of a relationship, we may be unwilling to commit to more than a single evening with this person we do not know very well. But as our investment in the relationship accumulates, our sense of commitment is likely to build as well.

High levels of investment and commitment are what allow people to "muddle through" the difficult periods that are an inevitable part of every relationship. As Lund puts it, during a time when benefits are few and costs are high, men and women may find it easier to make a small contribution to their investment than to leave the relationship. And every time they make this decision, their sense of commitment will become a little stronger.

To test her theory, Lund administered her Investment and Commitment scales, along with tests measuring love and rewards, to a sample of 129 men and women who were about to graduate from college. She reasoned that this milestone would strain many relationships and that this would provide her with the opportunity to determine if her scales could predict which relationships survived graduation and which relationships ended. Four months later, these men and women were contacted and questioned about the status of their relationships. As Lund predicted, the Investment and Commitment scales were the best predictors of the status of the relationship. Interestingly, although the measures of love and rewards were clearly related to relationship status, these tests were not nearly as accurate as Lund's tests in predicting which men and women had ended their relationships. Perhaps it is true that love is not enough. Even for those students who expressed strong feelings of love for their partners, the relationship was likely to end if investment and commitment were low.

Although the notion that certain barriers keep couples together even when love and rewards are ebbing seems slightly dreary, it may be a reason for optimism. Unlike love and rewards, which seem either to be there or not be there, we can exert some control over our investment and commitment. We may not be able to voluntarily increase our feelings of love for our partner when times are tough, but we can make a conscious decision to increase our investment. This idea has clear implications for couples who are experiencing difficult times. During a relationship crisis, most people tend to focus on how their partners have disappointed or hurt them. Perhaps a better strategy would be to use the items on Lund's test to come up with ideas about how one might invest in the relationship. Rather than point out your partner's shortcomings, arrange to spend a weekend together, surprise him or her with a gift, or pass up lunch with a friend in favor of your partner. This is an investment that could yield generous dividends.

Lund reported some interesting results regarding the effects of time on love and rewards along with investment and commitment. As you might expect, men and women's levels of investment and commitment increased as they moved from casually dating, to seriously involved, to exclusively involved, to engaged, and finally to married. However, this linear progression was not found for love and rewards. Love and rewards steadily increased up to the engaged point, but then there was a clear decline for the married men and women. Once again, this suggests that love may not be enough—investment and commitment are crucial.

Although it is clear that for most of us, our sense of commitment and our willingness to make investments in our relationships increase as time goes by, it is probably also the case that there are differences among people in their ability or willingness to invest and commit to a relationship. We have all known some people who simply are unwilling to invest much of their energy or their resources in any relationship. Also, there are people whose sense of commitment is so fragile that they will leave the first time they notice someone who might be more interesting. Lund's tests can give you a good sense of how similar you and your partner are in your levels of commitment and investment, but if you have a history of short-lived relationships, you might also find it useful to respond to the items a second time. This time answer them as you would have when you were in your most serious relationship. If you cannot imagine lending your car to this person for the weekend or giving up an afternoon with your friends to do a favor for him or her, your inability to have a long-term relationship may simply reflect your unwillingness to make the necessary investment. Of course, it could be equally instructive to ask a potential partner to do the same. If this person has never invested much in a relationship or developed a sense of commitment, it is unlikely that he or she will begin with you.

CHAPTER TWENTY

The Recreational Interests Inventory

Rate the degree you would be interested in participating in each of the following activities on a scale from 1 to 7, where a 1 means *not at all interested* and a 7 means *very interested*.

---

* Reprinted with permission of Michael Janda, Old Dominion University, Virginia Beach, Virginia.

____ 1. Playing softball

____ 2. Playing golf

____ 3. Being a spectator at a baseball game

____ 4. Hiking

____ 5. Bicycle riding

____ 6. Water sports (sailing, jet skiing, etc.)

____ 7. Playing tennis

____ 8. Horseback riding

____ 9. Going to the movies

____ 10. Going to a museum

____ 11. Attending a lecture on a topic that interests you

____ 12. Attending a play

____ 13. Reading and then discussing a book with a group of friends

____ 14. Attending a concert

____ 15. Viewing a touring art exhibit

____ 16. Touring a famous house or garden

____ 17. Attending a party

____ 18. Going out to dinner with a group of friends

____ 19. Having a barbecue with a group of friends

____ 20. Going out to a nightclub

____ 21. Having a group of friends over for a quiet evening

____ 22. Meeting and becoming acquainted with new people

____ 23. Going out dancing

Scale of 1 to 7
1 = Completely uninterested; 7 = Greatly interested

___ 24. Joining a special interest club (drama, literature, art, etc.)

___ 25. Gardening

___ 26. Shopping for items to place in my home

___ 27. Putting an addition on my house

___ 28. Working to make my home spotless

___ 29. Working on my home so that I can take pride in its appearance

___ 30. Working on an arts and crafts project

___ 31. Working on home improvements (painting the kitchen a different color, fixing a leaky faucet, etc.)

___ 32. Decorating my home for a holiday (Halloween, Christmas, etc.)

Scale of 1 to 7
1 = Completely uninterested; 7 = Greatly interested

SCORING

There are four subscales to the Recreational Interests Inventory. They are (1) Athletic (At), (2) Theoretical (Th), (3) Social (So), and (4) Home Improvement (Hi). To find your score on each subscale, simply add together the values of your responses. The items belonging to each subscale are as follows:

Athletic	Items 1–8
Theoretical	Items 9–16
Social	Items 17–24
Home Improvement	Items 25–32

HOW DO YOU COMPARE?

AT		TH		SO		HI		
M	**F**	**M**	**F**	**M**	**F**	**M**	**F**	**PERCENTILE**
42	37	39	40	44	44	30	36	85
38	33	35	36	40	40	26	32	70
32	29	31	32	36	36	22	28	50
28	25	27	28	32	32	18	24	30
24	21	23	24	28	28	14	20	15

High scores indicate higher levels of the interest in question. If, for example, you received a percentile score of 70 on Th, it means that 70 percent of people have less interest in the Theoretical than do you.

For more information, see D.R. Hawley, "Couples in Crisis. Using Self-Report Instruments in Marriage Counseling," *Pastoral Psychology* 43 (1994): 93–103.

Amy Gutterman, Anthony Macera, and Stephanie Caruthers developed the norms for this test.

ABOUT THE RECREATIONAL INTERESTS INVENTORY

Which cliché is more accurate: birds of a feather flock together or opposites attract? Psychologists have studied this question for decades, and the clear answer is that birds of a feather flock together.

That the evidence is so overwhelming might surprise you because most people seem to think that they are attracted to their opposites. And indeed, we all tend to find the exotic and unusual interesting and can point to relationships that we have had in which the other person was very different. But while people who are very different may hold some transitory appeal for us, the odds are much better that we will stay with a person who shares the same interests.

The most vivid example I can think of to illustrate the importance of similarity of interests involved a young couple I saw in therapy who, after only eighteen months of marriage, concluded their relationship was in trouble. One of the questions I asked them concerned the kinds of things they enjoyed doing together. They agreed there was nothing that fit this description. The wife complained that her husband's only interest was in playing softball with his friends, and the husband grumbled that if his wife had her way, they would do nothing with their free time but go shopping.

At the beginning of therapy, many couples have difficulty in saying anything nice about each other, so I asked the question in a slightly different way: "When was the last time you did enjoy doing something together?" They both thought long and hard before the husband was able to provide an answer with which his wife agreed: "We enjoyed planning the wedding together."

When feelings of romantic love are at their peak and you are convinced you have found the person with whom you want to spend the rest of your life, it may seem inconceivable that you would ever need to have some specific activity to motivate you to spend time with your partner. When the relationship is new and the bloom is still on the rose, simply being together is enough; it doesn't matter what you are doing as long as you are with each other. But the intensity of romantic love inevitably fades, and there will come a time when you will wonder what the two of you can do together that you will both enjoy. Without such common interests, it will become increasingly difficult to see the point of staying together. If he spends every evening playing softball with his buddies and she spends all her free time at the mall with her friends, the day will come when one or both of them will wonder whether they would enjoy being with someone else.

Donn Byrne, the psychologist who did much of the pioneering research in this area, found that there was a strong, linear relationship between similarity of interests and attitudes and interpersonal attraction. This means that as the percentage of similar attitudes and interests we have with another person increases, our attraction toward that person increases as well. We will be more attracted to a person with whom we have a great deal in common than to a person with whom we share a medium level of similar attitudes and interests. And, in turn, we will be more attracted to this person than to someone with whom we have very little in common. So, the more we have in common with a prospective partner, the better our odds are of making the relationship work.

Many of my students have found it difficult to believe that similarity of interests and attitudes is so important. They always have stories about how different they are from their partners or how different their parents are from each other. And they report that these relationships are quite satisfying despite these differences.

I think the answer to this apparent contradiction is that we are more likely to be aware of differences, rather than similarities, simply because differences are more noticeable. I know one couple who almost takes pride in the fact that they are so different. The woman is an extremely outgoing, social person who finds it uncomfortable when she doesn't have a project to occupy her time. Her husband, on the other hand, is a quiet man who enjoys nothing more than the prospect of a weekend without any obligations. While these differences have led to more than a few spirited discussions, they both find their relationship deeply satisfying and are completely committed to their life together.

My view is that it is their similarities, which are much more numerous than their differences, that account for the strong affection that bonds them to each other. They both are serious about their careers, they have nearly identical ideas about parenting, they see nearly every movie that comes out, and they love to go to baseball games, to name just a few of the things they have in common. If they were to make a complete list of their similar attitudes and interests, they would undoubtedly be surprised by its length simply because similarities rarely lead to the kind of discussions that differences do. They, like the rest of us, tend to take their similarities for granted while struggling to resolve their differences.

Byrne suggested two reasons why similar attitudes and interests are such a powerful force in interpersonal attraction. First, we like being around someone who has similar ideas because it serves to validate our own attitudes and interests. And second, we can expect to share mutually enjoyable activities with someone who has similar attitudes and interests. Maintaining a relationship with someone with quite different interests could become something of a chore if we had to continually defend our activities and somewhat lonely if we were to engage in these activities alone.

So how concerned should you be if you and your partner have completely different profiles on the Recreational Interest Inventory? It depends on two factors: your age and your flexibility. Interests can shift greatly over time, and I've known many people in their forties and fifties whose interests bore very little relation to what interested them in their twenties. When young couples are getting started with their adult life, the demands of this process are likely to provide them with much common ground. They may both be interested in finishing school, getting their careers started, buying their first house, caring for their first child, and keeping up with the nitty-gritty details of daily life. It is only as the children become older and self-sufficient that they have time to wonder about how they are going to spend their weekends together. Not having common interests to share can certainly be a problem for middle-aged couples, but psychological tests are not able to predict one's interests twenty years down the road. So, if you are a young adult and you and your partner have very different profiles, you have a great deal of time to develop common interests. And you will need them!

If you are beyond the early adulthood stage, it does become more complicated. If you and your partner have very different Recreational Interests profiles, you must evaluate how flexible you both can be. For whatever reason, women seem to be better at this than are men. Women often enjoy an activity simply because they are doing it with a partner, but men seem to require an inherent interest in the activity. I know many examples where the woman agreed to try activities such as camping, fishing, or golf simply so that she could share time with her partner.

Men, on the other hand, have more difficulty taking this approach (I confess I am guilty of this). I have yet to meet a man who was enthusiastic about, say, antique hunting simply because it was something he could share with his wife. Women who are contemplating a relationship with a man with very different interests must make their feelings clear. One woman I know, Trudy, said to her husband, Steve, "I know it is important to you to play golf with your friends on the weekend, but I don't think it is fair that we never have time to do something together." Steve was sufficiently flexible and sufficiently concerned about his wife's feelings to agree. He does take frequent weekends off from golf to accompany his wife on trips through small towns in search of unusual antiques—an activity he does not eagerly anticipate but one he participates in graciously because he knows it is important to Trudy.

On the other hand, I have known men who were unmoved by their partners' requests for more time together. One acquaintance told his wife that he would not give up weekend golf under any circumstances, and it was up to her to find something she enjoyed doing while he was on the course.

If you have reason to suspect your prospective partner is this type, you have to make a careful decision. Do not allow your rose-colored glasses to lull you into believing that he will change—it is more likely that he will only become more adamant as time goes by. You must decide if you can be happy with a partner who will be spending his Saturdays and Sundays away from you. If you are the independent type and have interests you can pursue alone or with friends, this might be okay with you. But if you are the sort of person who wants to have a relationship in which you share much of your free time with your partner, you will want to think long and hard before making a commitment to such a person.

CHAPTER TWENTY-ONE

The Money Ethic Scale

Rate each of the following statements as to the degree you agree or disagree with it, using the following scale:

1 = Strongly disagree
2 = Moderately disagree
3 = Neutral
4 = Moderately agree
5 = Strongly agree

* Reprinted with permission of Dr. Thomas Li-Ping Tang, Middle Tennessee State University, Murfreesboro, Tennessee.

___ 1. Money is an important factor in the lives of all of us.

___ 2. Money is good.

___ 3. Money is important.

___ 4. I value money very highly.

___ 5. Money is valuable.

___ 6. Money does not grow on trees.

___ 7. Money can buy you luxuries.

___ 8. Money is attractive.

___ 9. I think that it is very important to save some money.

___ 10. Money is the root of all evil.

___ 11. Money is evil.

___ 12. Money spent is money lost (wasted).

___ 13. Money is shameful.

___ 14. Money is useless.

___ 15. A penny saved is a penny earned.

___ 16. Money represents one's achievement.

___ 17. Money is the most important thing (goal) in my life.

___ 18. Money is a symbol of success.

___ 19. Money can buy everything.

___ 20. Money makes people respect you in the community.

___ 21. Money is honorable.

___ 22. Money will help you express your competence and abilities.

___ 23. Money can bring you many friends.

---

1 = Strongly disagree; 2 = Moderately disagree; 3 = Neutral;
4 = Moderately agree; 5 = Strongly agree

___ 24. I use my money very carefully.

___ 25. I budget my money very well.

___ 26. I pay my bills immediately in order to avoid interest or penalties.

___ 27. Money gives you autonomy and freedom.

___ 28. Money in the bank is a sign of security.

___ 29. Money can give you the opportunity to be what you want to be.

___ 30. Money means power.

1 = Strongly disagree; 2 = Moderately disagree; 3 = Neutral;
4 = Moderately agree; 5 = Strongly agree

Scoring

There are six subscales to the Money Ethic Scale. They are (1) Money Is Good (MG), (2) Money Is Evil (ME), (3) Achievement (A), (4) Money Brings Respect (MBR), (5) Budget (B), and (6) Money Brings Freedom/Power (MBFP). To find your score on each subscale, sum your responses to each item on each subscale. The items belonging to each subscale are as follows:

Money Is Good	Items 1–9
Money Is Evil	Items 10–15
Achievement	Items 16–19
Money Brings Respect	Items 20–23
Budget	Items 24–26
Money Brings Freedom/Power	Items 27–30

How Do You Compare?

MG	ME	A	MBR	B	MBFP	Percentile
56	21	16	20	18	23	85
53	19	14	18	16	21	70
50	17	11	15	14	19	50
47	15	8	13	12	16	30
44	13	6	10	10	14	15

High scores indicate a greater acceptance of the perspective in question. If, for instance, you received a percentile score of 70 on MG, 70 percent of people do not believe that Money is Good as strongly as you do.

For more information, see Thomas Li-Ping Tang, "The Development of a Short Money Ethic Scale: Attitudes Toward Money and Pay Satisfaction Revisited," *Personality and Individual Differences* 19 (1995): 809–816.

About the Money Ethic Scale

In every survey of divorcing couples, money problems are mentioned either first or second as reasons for the breakup. It seems sad that something as mundane as money can destroy the bond that brought two people together, but the reality is that money affects almost every aspect of our lives. And something with such a pervasive influence is likely to create a strain between two people who view money in different ways. Needless to say, your relationship is in for smoother sailing if you and your partner have similar ideas about money and how it should be used.

The Money Ethic Scale was developed to learn more about the basic ingredients of attitudes toward money. Thomas Li-Ping Tang, the scale's author, concluded that there were five dimensions to the money ethic—the five dimensions for which you could derive scores. Our general principle that birds of a feather flock together applies to these five dimensions, but there is at least one important exception: Couples who both have high scores on the Achievement and Money Brings Respect dimensions (they tend to correlate with each other) and low scores on the Budget dimension may be headed for trouble.

The explanation for this may be obvious, but let me provide you with an example. Ron and Janet both believed that their money symbolized their achievement, and they both derived much of their self-esteem from the trappings of success. They both had good jobs—together they earned well into six figures—and neither of them was especially interested in, or good at, budgeting. When friends or relatives visited their home for the first time, they were given the grand tour, and both Ron and Janet became skilled at working the price of many of their possessions into the conversation. Ron even went so far as to show people the contents of his freezer, which was always packed with the most expensive cuts of meat.

Because their self-aggrandizing talk was so obnoxious, many of their friends secretly chuckled when Ron and Janet had to declare bankruptcy. Since Ron's income had been increasing dramatically for several years, neither of them worried about how much credit they were using in their quest to acquire all the trappings of wealth. They assumed that their income would always increase at the same rate and that within a few years, once they had everything they wanted, they could think about paying off their bills. Life often works out differently than we had planned, and to this maxim Ron and Janet were no exception. During a mild recession, Ron's income dropped dramatically, and they could not come close to making their minimum monthly payments. Within a year, they were forced to sell their house at a substantial loss and to declare bankruptcy to get out from under their mountain of debt. Ron and Janet were humiliated by their setback. They could not face their friends without their possessions, so they moved halfway across the country for a fresh start.

Despite the importance of having at least one budgeter in the family, the most common scenario I have seen in my practice is when one partner is high on the Budget dimension and the other is high on the Money Brings Respect, or self-esteem, dimension. Barry and

Michelle fell into this category. Michelle, a stay-at-home mom, handled the family finances and was continually distraught to see Barry's credit card charges come in because she knew it meant that there would not be enough money left to pay all the bills. She tried everything to get Barry to change his ways. She pleaded with him, screamed at him, cried more times than she could remember, and even tried giving him the silent treatment when his bills rolled in. Nothing worked. Barry always promised to do better, but his self-esteem was so fragile that he was helpless to control his spending. He had to prove to his friends and to the world that he could afford anything he wanted. The problem was, of course, that he really could not.

Detecting potential problems with the Money Ethic Scale can be tricky. As the two examples above suggest, there are a couple of clear danger signals. If either you or your partner has extremely high scores on Money Brings Respect and Achievement, you may be in for some problems. But, as always, there are exceptions. Sam measured his self-worth in terms of money and the material, but he had little interest in buying anything. He did not have time to spend much money because he was so busy earning it. The checks he turned over to his wife, Vera, were sufficient for her to furnish their house exquisitely while staying current with all their bills. So Vera and Sam never had an argument about money, although Sam's long hours at the office left Vera feeling lonely and isolated at times.

Perhaps the best result would be for both you and your partner to have moderate scores on all five dimensions. Based on my experience with counseling couples, problems are likely to occur when one of the partners has extreme attitudes on any dimension, regardless of which one it is. One of the more unusual examples involves Ted and Monica. Ted was more than responsible with his money. He was never late in paying any of his bills, and he was putting 15 percent of his salary away in a tax-sheltered retirement plan. But Monica was perhaps the most extreme budgeter I have ever met. Although her financial situation would be the envy of most people, she refused to spend the money to mail her bills. Every month she would spend two to three hours driving around the city to make these payments in person to save the cost of stamps. Unfortunately for Ted, she expected him to be just as frugal as she was. Now, ten years after I first met them, they have made a number of compromises, but they still occasionally exchange harsh words about money issues.

Tang's research with his Money Ethic Scale did reveal something that is important to keep in mind: People's attitudes toward money generally change as they grow older. Tang found that younger respondents had higher scores on the Money Is Evil dimension and lower scores on the Budget dimension than did their older counterparts. Perhaps this should not be surprising. I know that when I was a college student, I had a disdain for the material. And I had no credit, so budgeting was not much of an issue. The point, though, is that you must consider your age, as well as your partner's, when evaluating your scores on this test. A low score on the Budget dimension for a twenty-two-year-old does not mean the same thing as a low score for a forty-three-year-old. Twenty-two-year-olds are likely to change. Forty-three-year-olds, on the other hand, are probably firmly set in their ways.

Even if you and your partner have very different Money Ethic profiles, your situation is far from hopeless. As always, your future together depends on your willingness to compromise and find solutions that both of you can live with. The most common solution I have seen is for budgeters to give their profligate partners an "allowance." Keith's wife Ellen used to drive him crazy with her habit of shopping when they did not have enough money in the bank to pay their monthly bills. They sat down together, worked out a budget, and agreed that Ellen could have a certain amount of money each month to spend as she pleased without having to account for it. She opened a separate checking account for this money because her lackadaisical record keeping, which resulted in frequent bounced checks, also annoyed her husband. For this to work, Ellen had to acknowledge that she had been acting irresponsibly. She did admit this, and she came to like the "allowance" idea because it eliminated the heated discussions she had with Keith about many of her purchases.

If you and your partner have frequent disagreements about money, this test is a good place to begin when trying to understand why you have such different views. If you believe you need professional assistance, it is possible to obtain such help at no cost in most good-size cities. Your credit bureau or chamber of commerce may be able to refer you to a financial counselor.

CHAPTER TWENTY-TWO

The Child-Rearing Disagreements Scale

and the Children's Exposure to Marital Disagreements Scale

THE CHILD-REARING DISAGREEMENTS SCALE

Couples with children find many different topics to disagree on. Please indicate how often, during the last six months, you and your spouse have had irritating disagreements in the following areas by entering a number from 1 to 6 in the blank next to each item, where a 1 means *no disagreement* and a 6 means *consistent disagreement*.

During the last six months, my spouse has irritated me by doing the following:

---

* Reprinted with permission of Dr. Ernest N. Jouriles, University of Houston, Houston, Texas.

___ 1. Letting our child make a mess all over the house

___ 2. Buying too many or too expensive toys

___ 3. Babying our child

___ 4. Being too lenient with our child

___ 5. Expecting our child to follow rules that are too much for his/her age

___ 6. Being too casual about our child's clothes, grooming, dirty face, and so forth

___ 7. Being too quick to discipline our child

___ 8. Not keeping a close enough eye on our child's whereabouts

___ 9. Being too slow about seeing a doctor for our child's colds, injuries, and so forth

___ 10. Pushing our child to learn too much at an early age

___ 11. Being too casual with our child about behavior that could lead to accidents

___ 12. Not taking an equal hand in disciplining our child

___ 13. Being too tired (reasonably or not) to spend time with our child when he/she wanted

___ 14. Doing the easy or fun things but not too many of the hard or boring things in child care

___ 15. Having to be asked to do a little more with our child when I am dead on my feet or not feeling well

___ 16. Criticizing my child-rearing practices from the sidelines (i.e., more comments than help)

___ 17. Letting some bit of misbehavior go on and on until I finally do something about it myself

___ 18. Being hardheaded about certain aspects of childrearing

___ 19. Implying that some of our child's misbehavior is partly my fault

___ 20. Not sticking to agreements we made about child care or childrearing

___ 21. Not trusting my judgment in certain aspects of childrearing

Scale of 1 to 6
1 = No disagreement; 6 = Consistent disagreement

SCORING

To calculate your score on this scale, simply add the values of your responses.

HOW DO YOU COMPARE?

SCORE	PERCENTILE
49	85
44	70
38	50
33	30
28	15

High scores indicate greater disagreement about childrearing. If, for instance, you had a percentile score of 70, it means that 70 percent of people report less disagreement than you do about childrearing.

THE CHILDREN'S EXPOSURE TO MARITAL DISAGREEMENTS SCALE

We have found that families differ widely in the extent to which their children are aware of family disagreements. Please indicate the extent to which your own child is aware of disagreements such as you have previously described. Use a 6-point scale, where a 1 means *never* and a 6 means *daily*.

During the last six months, our child has done the following:

___ 1. Been around us raising our voices at each other without it really being a quarrel

___ 2. Tried to join in, imitate, or take sides in a disagreement between me and my spouse

___ 3. Snuck around and listened to a fuss between me and my spouse

___ 4. Mistakenly thought my spouse and I were quarreling when we weren't

___ 5. Overheard my spouse complaining to me about my behavior

___ 6. Overheard me complain about my spouse's behavior

___ 7. Seen me or my spouse leave the room or storm off in the midst of a disagreement

___ 8. Been told to leave the room in order to avoid overhearing a disagreement

___ 9. Asked me and my spouse not to quarrel

___ 10. Been present when my spouse and I were sorting out a child-rearing disagreement

___ 11. Been fussed at by one of us when we were having some kind of disagreement

___ 12. Seen us stop in the middle of a fuss because he/she entered the room

SCORING

To obtain your score, simply add together the values for your responses.

HOW DO YOU COMPARE?

SCORE	PERCENTILE
24	85
22	70
19	50
16	30
14	15

High scores indicate that your children are exposed to higher levels of marital disagreements. If, for instance, you received a percentile score of 85, it means that 85 percent of people report that their children are exposed to less marital disagreement than are yours.

For more information, see Ernest N. Jouriles, Christopher M. Murphy, Annette M. Farris, David A. Smith, John E. Richters, and Everett Waters, "Marital Adjustment, Parental Disagreements about Childrearing, and Behavior Problems in Boys: Increasing the Specificity of Marital Assessment," *Child Development* 62 (1991): 1424–1433.

ABOUT THE CHILD-REARING DISAGREEMENTS SCALE AND THE CHILDREN'S EXPOSURE TO MARITAL DISAGREEMENTS SCALE

Perhaps no aspect of a relationship makes a greater demand on the couple to form a clear and effective partnership than caring for children. It is sadly ironic that so many men and women view having a baby as the ultimate sign of their love and then discover that caring for their child can provide the ultimate test of that love. Rearing children is hard. And if it is to be done effectively, both parents must be involved and must agree about the general principles they will follow.

Ernest Jouriles, a psychologist at the University of Houston, constructed two tests that are relevant to this issue. This first is called the Child-Rearing Disagreements Scale and it is comprised of the first twenty-one items. The second related test is the Children's Exposure to Marital Disagreements Scale, and it is comprised of the last twelve items. Jouriles's primary interest was in learning if parental disagreements about childrearing led to more problems with children's behavior. He, with the help of colleagues Christopher Murphy, Annette Farris, David Smith, John Richters, and Everett Waters, found evidence that this was the case. Parents with high scores on the Child-Rearing Disagreements Scale tended to have children who told lies, physically hurt other children, teased other children, used rude or dirty language, abused the property of others, got into trouble regularly, and disobeyed their parents' rules or instructions. As is always the case with behavioral research, these correlations were far from perfect. There were parents who had serious disagreements about childrearing who had well-behaved children, and there were parents who had formed a strong alliance regarding discipline, yet had unruly, difficult children.

Interestingly, Jouriles and his colleagues found that scores on the Children's Exposure to Marital Disagreements Scale had almost no relationship with the extent to which the couples reported problems with their children. The one exception was that compared with children who rarely heard their parents argue, children who were frequently exposed to their parents' disagreements used more rude and dirty language. Presumably, this resulted from hearing their parents use such language while arguing.

This finding is especially interesting because it is consistent with what many experts have advised parents over the years. The common wisdom is that children should not be sheltered from all parental disagreements. The belief is that by observing Mom and Dad having an argument, resolving it, and then making up, the child learns something important about how to manage conflict.

The key to this piece of advice is, of course, that the parents must be able to argue in a constructive fashion if they are to serve as good models for their children. I doubt that any child has ever learned anything useful by observing his or her parents screaming vile, hurtful epithets at each other.

I also believe there are certain topics to which no child should have to listen to the parents discuss. It may be helpful, for instance, for children to learn how their parents resolve problems about balancing the checkbook, washing the dishes, or taking the car in for repairs. But I cannot imagine what useful purpose it would serve for children to hear their parents argue about issues such as infidelity, substance abuse, or physical violence, to name just a few. Children want to view their parents as strong, capable, good people, and anything they hear that destroys their confidence in either parent can only be harmful. It will always be the case that children will discover their parents are not perfect (at least my kids have let me know of this discovery), but they do not want to learn that they are fatally flawed.

Human behavior is incredibly complex, and often what is most important is too subtle to be captured by any psychological test. I suspect that this is especially true when it comes to setting standards for children's behavior. Based upon my experience as a clinical psychologist, I have come to conclude that the specifics are not as important as the more general atmosphere in the home. Let me give you two brief examples.

First, Glen and Donna disagreed about almost everything when it came to their son, Gregory. Glen was a marine officer who firmly believed that the best way to treat his three-year-old son was as if he were a little man. "The more you expect of anyone, the more you will get" was his constant refrain. Donna, on the other hand, believed that children should be allowed to be children and that they would have a lifetime of adult responsibilities, so there was no reason to push them hard at such an early age.

Despite their frequent disagreements about discipline, Gregory was a well-adjusted, happy child. His parents loved him very much, and both were involved in his life. Gregory had learned that his mother would give him what he wanted, at times—for instance, when he skinned a knee or when a friend hurt his feelings. But he also enjoyed spending time with his father and always became involved in trying to accomplish the goals his father set for him.

Joe and Alicia, on the other hand, had very few disagreements about their daughter, Kelli. Alicia took most of the responsibility for their daughter's discipline, and Joe's major contribution was to periodically ask in an annoyed voice, "Can't you get her to be quiet?" Alicia worked full time and had almost all the responsibility of running the household. She was always tired, and because Kelli was an active child, Alicia frequently lost her patience and slapped her daughter in response to what often were minor infractions. Kelli's preschool teacher complained that Kelli was frequently disrespectful and physically aggressive with the other children.

The point is obvious. Glen and Donna loved their son and were willing to spend as much time with him as they could. While they had quite different views regarding the specifics of discipline, Gregory responded to their interest, caring, and love. Gregory quickly learned that his behavior would be held to a higher standard when his father was around, but he also learned that his father's discipline would be consistent and predictable. He had little difficulty in adapting.

Kelli's parents, on the other hand, failed to provide her with the consistency that would allow her to make sense of her world. She failed to learn that there was a connection between her behavior and what happened to her. She only knew that punishment depended largely on her mother's mood, and consequently, it seemed reasonable that she strike out at other children when they annoyed her. My experience strongly suggests that as long as both parents care about their child and both are involved in rearing the child, specific standards matter relatively little—within reason, of course.

For those of you in a second marriage, conflicts about discipline are especially critical. Surveys have found that problems with stepchildren are the number one reason why second marriages fail. The most common problem is that the biological parent resents what he or she perceives to be the partner's use of overly harsh punishment techniques. It is important to keep in mind that becoming a family takes time—it does not happen instantly as a result of a marriage ceremony. Stepparents would be well advised to stay in the background at first and then gradually assume the role of parent to the stepchildren.

The second most common problem is the flip side of the first—the biological parent refuses to allow his or her partner to impose any standards of behavior on the stepchildren. I have seen adults terrorized by children because the adults have learned that if they place any limits on their stepchildren's behavior, it will lead to a major argument with their partners. In these situations, it does not take long for the stepparent to feel like an outsider. And once that happens, the next logical step is to leave the relationship. Anyone contemplating a marriage in which one of the partners brings children to the relationship should make every effort to have an explicit understanding about their respective roles regarding discipline.

CHAPTER TWENTY-THREE

The Parenting Scale

At one time or another, all children misbehave or do things that could be harmful, that are "wrong," or that parents don't like. Examples include hitting someone, whining, throwing food, forgetting homework, not picking up toys, lying, having a tantrum, refusing to go to bed, wanting a cookie before dinner, running into the street, arguing back, and coming home late.

Parents have many different ways or styles of dealing with these types of problems. Following are items that describe some styles of parenting. For each of the situations, two courses of action are presented. In the blank beside each item, enter a number from 1 to 7 that provides your best estimate of where on this continuum your reaction would lie. Consider the following example:

____ At meal time…

I let my child decide how much to eat.   1–7   I decide how much my child eats.

---

* Reprinted with permission of Susan G. O'Leary, State University of New York at Stony Brook, Stony Brook, New York.

If you always allow your child to decide how much to eat, you would respond with a 1. If you always decide how much your child eats, you would respond with a 7. If your child decides how much to eat half the time and you decide half the time, you would respond with a 4, and so on.

____ 1. When my child misbehaves...

| I do something right away. | 1–7 | I do something about it later. |

____ 2. Before I do something about a problem...

| I give my child several reminders or warnings. | 1–7 | I use only one reminder or warning. |

____ 3. When I'm upset or under stress...

| I am picky and on my child's back. | 1–7 | I am no more picky than usual. |

____ 4. When I tell my child not to do something...

| I say very little. | 1–7 | I say a lot. |

____ 5. When my child pesters me...

| I can ignore the pestering. | 1–7 | I can't ignore the pestering. |

____ 6. When my child misbehaves...

| I usually get into a long argument with my child. | 1–7 | I don't get into an argument. |

____ 7. I threaten to do things that...

| I am sure I can carry out. | 1–7 | I know I won't actually do. |

____ 8. I am the kind of parent that...

> sets limits on what   1–7   lets my child do
> my child is allowed   what he or she
> to do.   wants.

____ 9. When my child misbehaves...

> I give my child   1–7   I keep my talks
> a long lecture.   short and to the
>   point.

____ 10. When my child misbehaves...

> I raise my voice or yell. 1–7   I speak to my child
>   calmly.

____ 11. If saying no doesn't work right away...

> I take some other   1–7   I keep talking and
> kind of action.   try to get through to
>   my child.

____ 12. When I want my child to stop doing something...

> I firmly tell my   1–7   I coax or beg my
> child to stop.   child to stop.

____ 13. When my child is out of my sight...

> I often don't know   1–7   I always have a
> what my child is doing.   good idea of what
>   my child is doing.

____ 14. After there's been a problem with my child...

> I often hold a grudge.   1–7   things get back to
>   normal quickly.

____ 15. When we're not at home...

> I handle my child the   1–7   I let my child get
> way I do at home.   away with a lot more.

____ 16. When my child does something I don't like...

> I do something   1–7   I often let it go.
> about it.

_____17. When there's a problem with my child…

things build up,   1–7   things don't get out
and I do things   of hand.
I don't mean to do.

_____18. When my child misbehaves, I spank, slap, grab, or
hit my child…

never or rarely.   1–7   most of the time.

_____19. When my child doesn't do what I ask…

I often let it go or end 1–7   I take some other
up doing it myself.   action.

_____20. When I give a fair threat or warning…

I often don't carry it out. 1–7   I always do what I
said.

_____21. If saying no doesn't work…

I take some other   1–7   I offer my child
kind of action.   something nice so
that he/she will
behave.

_____22. When my child misbehaves…

I handle it without   1–7   I get so frustrated or
getting upset.   angry that my child
can see I'm upset.

_____23. When my child misbehaves…

I make my child tell   1–7   I say no or take
me why he/she did it.   some other action.

_____24. If my child misbehaves and then acts sorry…

I handle the problem   1–7   I let it go that time.
like I usually would.

_____25. When my child misbehaves…

I rarely use bad   1–7   I almost always use
language or curse.   bad language.

____26. When I say my child can't do something...

    I let my child do   1–7   I stick to
    it anyway.   what I said.

____27. When I have to handle a problem...

    I tell my child that   1–7   I don't say that I'm
    I'm sorry.   sorry about it.

____28. When my child does something I don't like, I insult my child, say mean things, or call my child names...

    never or rarely.   1–7   most of the time.

____29. If my child talks back or complains when I handle a problem...

    I ignore the   1–7   I give my child a
    complaining and stick   talk about not
    to what I said.   complaining.

____30. If my child gets upset when I say no...

    I back down and   1–7   I stick to what I
    give in to my child.   said.

Scoring

There are three subscales to the Parenting Scale. They are (1) Laxness (L), (2) Overreactivity (O), and (3) Verbosity (V). To find your score for each subscale, simply add the values of your responses. Add the values of all your responses to calculate your total score. The items that belong to each subscale are as follows:

L	O	V	Misc.
7	3*	2*	1
8	6*	4	5
12	9*	7	13*
15	10*	9	27*
16	14*	11	
19*	17*	23*	
20*	18	29	
21	22		
24	25		
26*	28		
30*			

* The items marked with an asterisk are reverse scored
(i.e., 1 = 7, 2 = 6, 3 = 5, 4 = 4, 5 = 3, 6 = 2, and 7 = 1).

How Do You Compare?

L	O	V	Total	Percentile
35	31	29	96	85
30	28	26	87	70
26	24	22	78	50
22	20	18	69	30
17	17	15	60	15

High scores indicate more ineffective parenting techniques. If, for instance, you received a percentile score of 70, it means that 70 percent of people use more effective parenting techniques than do you.

For more information, see David S. Arnold, Susan G. O'Leary, Lisa S. Wolff, and Maureen M. Acker, "The Parenting Scale: A Measure of Dysfunctional Parenting in Discipline Situations," *Psychological Assessment* 5 (1993): 137–144.

ABOUT THE PARENTING SCALE

Couples with strong relationships not only present a united front for their children, they both are interested and effective disciplinarians. If one parent is either disinterested or ineffective when it comes to discipline, the partner is likely to resent having to shoulder the lion's share of the burden of rearing the children. If you are having disagreements with your partner about how to deal with your children, an excellent place to start is by sitting down and completing together the Parenting Scale. Developed by Susan O'Leary and her colleagues David Arnold, Lisa Wolff, and Maureen Acker, all of whom are at the State University of New York at Albany, this scale has evolved from a careful program of research that has compared effective parents with their less effective counterparts. By comparing your scores and discussing the issues raised by the items on the test, the odds are good that both you and your partner can learn to be more effective parents. The reward will be in having a better relationship with both your partner and your children.

O'Leary and her colleagues point out that 10 percent of elementary school children are diagnosed as suffering from conduct disorders. These include problems with acting out, oppositional behavior, and aggressive behavior. As these children grow older, they are likely to develop more severe problems such as drug and alcohol abuse, family violence, crime, and assorted psychiatric disorders. These researchers have presented evidence that parents of children with conduct disorders, as compared with parents of typical children, tend to rely on lengthy verbal harangues when dealing with misbehavior. These parents are also likely to be submissive, ambiguous, and inconsistent with their children, and they often reinforce oppositional behavior with attention, softening of commands, or coaxing.

It is critical to use effective parenting techniques from the beginning because once the child reaches adolescence, it will not make much difference what the parents do. A number of research studies have found that helping parents of preschool children to use more effective parenting techniques can make a substantial difference in the children's behavior in classroom settings. Similar studies with the parents of adolescent children with conduct disorders have found that changes in parenting techniques have very little effect. The critical age for children appears to be from two to three years. Parents must be prepared from the very beginning to be effective disciplinarians if they are to reduce the odds that their children will have behavioral problems when they enter school.

The items on the Parenting Scale convey what research psychologists have learned about ineffective discipline. The first issue concerns what O'Leary calls Laxness. Laxness describes situations in which parents ignore their own rules, often in response to the child's objections. An example would be the parent who tells the child it is time for bed and then, when the child objects with a temper tantrum, says, "Okay, but only fifteen minutes more." An important guideline for parents is to be consistent. If bedtime is 8:00 P.M., then the child must learn that it is 8:00 P.M. no matter how much he or she argues, begs, or cries. It would be an unusual child who, after a week of two of consistent and firm enforcement of the rule, would not follow it willingly.

The second characteristic of ineffective parenting is Overreactivity. Parents who allow themselves to become so upset and angry that they yell and scream, or even hit or slap the child, rarely get the results they want.

Ann was a screamer. When her two-year-old daughter Tiffany misbehaved, Ann would yell at her to stop. This process would escalate during the day until Ann reached her breaking point and would slap her daughter on the behind, often for what turned out to be a minor infraction. What Tiffany learned, however, was not what Ann was trying to teach her. Tiffany learned that her mother's screaming did not mean much of anything. She could continue to do what she wanted and expect to get whacked at some point during the day. But the connection between her behavior and getting whacked never became clear to Tiffany.

The third characteristic of ineffective parenting is Verbosity. Two- and three-year-old children do not respond to reason or guilt. Effective parents realize there is no point in trying to explain to children why they should behave appropriately; they set the contingencies for misbehavior and enforce them consistently with relatively little discussion. So if their two-year-old is marching to the nearest electrical outlet with fork in hand, a single verbal admonition would be issued. If the child continued to approach the outlet, the effective parent would then administer the punishment. It could be a swat on the behind or a fifteen-minute time-out, but it would be administered in a matter-of-fact way, without anger.

There were a few items on the Parenting Scale that did not fall into one of the three categories mentioned. Two of these strike me as especially important. The first is "When my child misbehaves . . . I do something right away" versus "I do something about it later." Toddlers do not respond to delayed punishment. The frustrated mother who tells her three-year-old "Wait until your father gets home" will only succeed in teaching the child to fear Dad. With young children, punishment must be immediate if it is to be effective.

The second of these items is "When I handle a problem . . . I tell my child I'm sorry about it" versus "I don't say I'm sorry." I admit to having made my share of mistakes as a parent, but I still remember my incredulity when a friend of mine spoke sharply to his four-year-old daughter, Jamie, when she misbehaved. Jamie, who obviously had not been the subject of effective parenting, responded, "Don't you yell at me!" My friend immediately apologized. As you might guess, Jamie was a real terror.

One thing you may have noticed about the Parenting Scale is that O'Leary and her colleagues, unlike so many experts, do not use it to suggest the standards parents should set for their children. Specific standards depend on the values of the parents, and no mental health professional should presume to tell parents what values they should enforce. For instance, I was fairly lenient about the movies my children were allowed to see, but I had a friend who would not let her children see anything other than G-rated movies until they were teenagers. I did not see the point because all our children heard much worse language on the school bus, but I would never suggest to my friend that she was being overly strict. Indeed, I admired her for being completely consistent.

So, be wary of any expert who suggests what parents should teach their children. This is clearly your domain. But on the other hand, when serious researchers, such as O'Leary and her colleagues, have something to say about effective techniques for teaching your children what you would like them to learn, they are well worth listening to.

CHAPTER TWENTY-FOUR

The General Marital Disagreements Scale

Most couples find that they have disagreements at times. Please indicate the degree of agreement or disagreement that you and your spouse have had during the last six months in each of the following areas by entering a number from 1 to 6 in the blank next to each item, where a 1 means *no disagreement* and a 6 means *consistent disagreement*.

---

* Reprinted with permission of Dr. Ernest N. Jouriles, University of Houston, Houston, Texas.

___ 1. Handling family finances

___ 2. How to spend holidays and free time

___ 3. Choice of friends

___ 4. Employment and career decisions

___ 5. Amount of time spent together

___ 6. Household tasks and maintenance

___ 7. Warmth and affection in our relationship

___ 8. Modern versus old-fashioned attitudes

___ 9. Fair sharing of workload between partners

___ 10. Time for self versus time with family

Scale of 1 to 6
1 = No disagreement; 6 = Consistent disagreement

SCORING

To calculate your score on this scale, simply add the values of your responses.

HOW DO YOU COMPARE?

SCORE	PERCENTILE
30	85
27	70
23	50
19	30
16	15

High scores indicate higher levels of marital disagreement. If, for instance, you received a percentile score of 85, it means that 85 percent of people report less marital disagreement than do you.

For more information, see Ernest N. Jouriles, Christopher M. Murphy, Annette M. Farris, David A. Smith, John E. Richters, and Everett Waters, "Marital Adjustment, Parental Disagreements about Childrearing, and Behavior Problems in Boys: Increasing the Specificity of Marital Assessment," *Child Development* 62 (1991): 1424–1433.

ABOUT THE GENERAL MARITAL DISAGREEMENTS SCALE

It will come as no surprise to learn that the extent to which couples have disagreements plays an important role in their level of overall satisfaction with their relationship. Indeed, couples who seek therapy for their relationship problems are likely to receive a high score on the General Marital Disagreements Scale. Ernest Jouriles, a psychologist at the University of Houston, developed this test to provide a brief, efficient measure of the level of conflict within a relationship. His primary interest was in the potential effects of marital conflict on the adjustment of children, and he found that couples with high scores reported more behavioral problems with their children.

Although it is true that generally there is a strong relationship between level of disagreements and overall satisfaction with a relationship, a number of family researchers have found that this relationship does not hold for all couples. Consider the case of Michael and Cindy, a couple I saw in therapy a few years ago. They agreed they had relatively few disagreements, yet Cindy was extremely unhappy in their marriage and had already told Michael she intended to divorce him. She agreed to try therapy for a few months before moving out of their apartment.

It was very difficult for Cindy to articulate the reasons for her unhappiness, other than to say she felt lonely and isolated despite the fact that she and Michael spent much of their free time together. After several sessions of therapy, it became clearer that Cindy was not sure Michael really cared about her. She expressed it this way: "Much of the time I have the feeling that it wouldn't matter who he was married to as long as he had someone to cook his dinner and someone with whom he could go to movies and have sex. Sure, we get along fine, and we hardly ever argue. But there doesn't seem to be any real reason for us to be together. I wish that just once he would tell me why he wants to stay married to me."

Michael and Cindy came from very different backgrounds. Michael's parents had a stable marriage, but they essentially led separate lives. Michael vowed that his marriage would be better, and in his mind, he had been successful because he spent so much of his free time with his wife. While he loved Cindy dearly, it was difficult for him to put his feelings into words. Anyway, he believed his actions spoke much louder than mere words.

Cindy's father left the family when she was a young child, and her notion of what marriage should be like was based on television and movie relationships. She expected large dosages of emotional intimacy and a husband who regularly told her how much he loved her and how important she was to him. When she did not hear these words, she concluded that she was missing something important, something that other women had in their lives and that she could find with another man.

Michael and Cindy's case was easier than most. Michael had to learn that as admirable as his attempts to show his love for Cindy were, it was even more important to show it in a way that was meaningful to her. And Cindy had to appreciate that love and caring can be expressed in a number of ways. To feel more secure and loved, she needed to interpret Michael's wanting to spend time with her and help her with the household chores as evidence that he cared about her.

The moral of this story is twofold. First, not all couples with low scores on the General Marital Disagreements Scale will be happy in their relationships. And second, if this is the case for you, it is critical that you articulate what it is you believe is missing from your relationship. Because Michael and Cindy had few arguments and because he was trying his best to make her happy, he only felt frustrated when she talked about her unhappiness without being explicit about what she wanted.

Although Jouriles did not collect evidence about the relationship between the level of disagreement and the number of arguments a couple has, my experience, both personally and professionally, is that the two issues may not always correspond. Although those couples with few disagreements clearly have a big head start in making their relationships work, it is possible for a couple to have a high level of disagreement but to have relatively few arguments. Successful couples with a high level of disagreement are those who have learned to make compromises and to manage conflict in a constructive fashion. Also, it is the case that even couples who argue regularly can have satisfying relationships. One interesting finding from research dealing with relationship satisfaction is that neither the number of arguments nor the number of sexual encounters predicts marital satisfaction. But the number of arguments relative to the number of sexual encounters does predict satisfaction. The researchers found that the critical ratio was three to one. Couples who made love three times for each argument they had were likely to be happy in their relationship. Relationships can withstand relatively high levels of conflict as long as they experience even higher levels of positive experiences. So the next time you do have an argument with your partner, you would be well advised to make love three times before you allow yourself to exchange harsh words again.

One item on the General Disagreements Scale is especially interesting and deserves further discussion. This is Item 8, which asked about modern versus old-fashioned attitudes. This item can have a variety of meanings, but one of the possible implications concerns sex roles. That is, does your relationship follow the old-fashioned model of a male-dominated marriage or the more current model of an equal-partners or sharing relationship?

The issue of sex roles and romantic/marital relationships has been the focus of much research that has produced some surprising findings. First, many men and women have found that they are not happy living with the type of person they were initially attracted to. While most married women want a partner who will help with the household chores and change their share of diapers, they may not be especially interested in such a man when they first meet him. One of my graduate students did her thesis in this area, and she found that college women had little interest in going out with the type of man who expressed a desire to work part time so that he could equally share child-rearing responsibilities. College women wanted to meet the type of man, described as aggressive and self-confident, who began his own construction company and by working fourteen-hour days had made it a huge success.

Men are not any clearer about what they want. If they find a woman physically attractive, they are likely to find all kinds of reasons why she is the right person for them. While men love to date the type of woman who is soft and cuddly and who makes them feel as if they are the center of her universe, they find her cloying five years later when she demands more of their attention.

Research has found that marriages in which both partners view the relationship as one between equal partners are likely to be the most satisfying. Interestingly, though, there are still a number of couples who subscribe to the man-as-head-of-the-household view of marriage. Indeed, women who viewed their role as one that required a great deal of deference were happier when they were married to a man who saw himself as "the boss" than when they were married to a man who did not want to take on the lion's share of the responsibility. It is important to know precisely what it is you want before you make a commitment.

If you did have a score higher than the 85 percentile of the General Marital Disagreements Scale, you have a lot of work to do if you are to make your relationship last. It is extremely difficult to change either your own or your partner's feelings about the issues involved, so the more fruitful strategy is to work out a series of compromises. You can use the items on the scale as a framework for your discussions. For instance, if you disagree about choice of friends, you might compromise by agreeing to spend one evening with your partner's friends for every evening the two of you spend with your friends. Or, you might agree to spend more time with your partner's friends if your partner agrees to take on more responsibility for household tasks. Remember, no one gets everything he or she wants from a relationship. The key to having a successful relationship is for both people to have the sense that they are getting more from it than they are giving up.

Epilogue

SOME FINAL THOUGHTS

I hope that by taking the tests in this book you learned something about yourself that you consider important. All of these tests fall into the category of self-report tests, so the chances are good that you were already aware—at least, at some level—of the imperfections that may have been standing in the way of your forming satisfying and lasting romantic relationships. But tests such as these can often serve to focus your thoughts, to help you think about these issues a little more clearly. I hope this was the case for you.

As I said several times throughout the book, I firmly believe these tests are potentially most useful if they serve to generate open and honest discussions between you and your partner. Most of us believe that we know our partner better than we actually do. We assume that we can tell what our partner is thinking or feeling by attending to subtle cues, such as facial expression or body language. But most of us will be surprised a number of times (and I am not excluded here, Meredith's responses surprised me dozens of times) by our partner's responses to these tests. That we can be surprised by how our partner views himself or herself, us, or our situation is evidence that we cannot make assumptions about what motives our partner may have had for some seemingly thoughtless or hurtful act or about what he or she may be thinking at any particular time. And it is these erroneous assumptions that can lead to conflict.

Meredith taught me another lesson about the value of taking these tests with your partner. She was surprised by my responses dozens of times as well, and for many of these instances, she made a strong case that my behavior was not especially consistent with my test responses. Clearly, I had a few blind spots of my own, so it is likely that you might learn about a few of your blind spots as well. Blind spots are no more helpful to a relationship than are erroneous assumptions.

There is one point that I made at the beginning of the book but that is so important that I want to repeat it. Almost without exception, these tests were developed to be used by behavioral scientists in their research dealing with relationships. They were not constructed to be used to categorize or make decisions about individuals. Therefore, if you scored extremely high or extremely low on any of the tests, it does not mean that you lack the potential to be a good romantic partner. Yes, extreme scores may mean that there are things about yourself that you might want to change and that you have more obstacles than most to overcome if you want to have a satisfying romantic relationship, but they DO NOT mean that you have reason to give up hope of finding a relationship that is right for you. Please use the book as intended: as a guide to help you better understand yourself and your relationship.

I hope you enjoyed the process of taking the tests and discussing the results with that important person in your life. My goal was to put together a book that was as entertaining as it was instructive. After all, self-discovery can be fun, and developing a closer, more intimate relationship with your partner can be especially gratifying.

Good luck, and may your relationship be both gratifying and eternal.